"I have long been waiting for a book about The Book that combines readability with scholarly accuracy. In *The Story of Scripture* Plummer has provided us with answers about the nature of the Bible that are accessible and substantive and prove helpful to Christians and non-Christians alike."

—Sam Storms, Senior Pastor,
Bridgeway Church,
Oklahoma City, OK

"Eminently understandable, crystal clear, and thoroughly engaging."

—Bruce A. Ware,
Professor of Christian Theology,
The Southern Baptist Theological Seminary

"These booklets from Rob Plummer are a gift to the church of Jesus Christ. Few can take the fruits of faithful scholarship and serve them in an eminently accessible form for the benefit of the church. Rob Plummer succeeds admirably at this very point. These booklets have my highest recommendation."

—Jason C. Meyer, Pastor for Preaching & Vision,
Bethlehem Baptist Church,
Minneapolis, MN

The STORY *of* SCRIPTURE

How We Got Our Bible and Why We Can Trust It

ROBERT L. PLUMMER

Kregel
Publications

Printed in the United States of America

13 14 15 16 17 / 5 4 3 2 1

Contents

Introduction

Never in the history of the world have so many resources existed to help Christians understand the Bible. It's surprising, then, that many modern-day Christians lack even a rudimentary understanding of the Bible's contents, organization, and history. Rather than being prepared "to give an answer" (1 Peter 3:15) to persons who doubt the Bible's accuracy or authority, Christians find themselves bewildered and intimidated. It is my hope that this book will be one small step in equipping God's people to understand his Word, trust it, and explain it to others.

This seven-chapter study was condensed from my larger work, *40 Questions About Interpreting the Bible* (Kregel, 2010). For this new format, the material has been updated and reworked slightly. The main benefit of this condensed layout is to provide a brief, accurate, and affordable resource for individuals, churches, or small groups interested in foundational questions about the Bible.

For persons leading a study based on this book, additional free resources (PowerPoint files, answers to discussion questions, lessson plans, etc.) may be found under the "Resources" tab at www.robplummer.com.

I want to express thanks to Michael Graham for proofreading and to my former professors, Robert Stein and Mark Seifrid, who obeyed 2 Timothy 2:2.

CHAPTER 1

The Nature and Purpose of the Bible

Most people who pick up this book will be familiar with the Bible. Yet, I am including this first, basic chapter for two reasons: (1) There will be some people who happen upon this book who have little to no knowledge of the Christian Scriptures. If that describes you, there is no better place to start than right here. (2) Even people who have spent many years reading the Bible can benefit from returning to the fundamentals. It is my hope that the discussion below will be understandable to people ignorant of the Bible but not so simplistic as to be of no benefit to those already well versed in the Christian Scriptures.

Overview of the Bible

The Bible is a collection of writings that Christians consider uniquely inspired and authoritative. While it is one unified book, the Bible is also a compilation of sixty-six smaller books, or literary works. These works, produced by men of various historical time periods, backgrounds, personalities, and cultures, claim the Holy Spirit as the ultimate authority and safeguard behind their writing. As 2 Timothy 3:16 asserts, "All Scripture is God-breathed."

The Bible can be divided into two large sections—the Old Testament and the New Testament. The word *testament* comes from the Latin word *testamentum*, meaning "covenant" or "agreement." Thus, in its basic division, the Bible records two covenantal relationships between God and humanity. The first (old) covenant relationship was ratified at Mount Sinai between God and the Jewish nation (Exod. 19–31). This covenant was anticipatory and pointed to a new covenant, promised in Jeremiah 31:31, when God would draw a people to himself from all nations and write his words on their hearts (Isa. 49:6). In fact, this new covenant was in reality nothing other than a fulfillment of the many saving promises God had made throughout history—that Satan would be crushed by a human descendant of Eve (Gen. 3:15), that through Abraham's offspring all the nations of the world would be blessed (Gen. 22:18), etc.

Within the Old Testament are thirty-nine books of various genres (historical narratives, proverbs, poetry, psalms, etc.). The New Testament contains twenty-seven books, again made up of various literary types (historical narratives, letters, parables, etc.) See chapter 2 for more information on the organization of the Bible (that is, order of books, origin of chapter and verse divisions, etc.).

The Purpose of the Bible

The Bible itself is evidence of one of its main claims—that is, that the God who made the heavens, earth, and sea, and everything in them is a communicator who delights to reveal himself to wayward humans. We read in Hebrews 1:1–2, "In the past God spoke to our forefathers through the prophets at many times and in various ways, but in these last days he has spoken to us by his Son, whom he appointed heir of all things, and through whom he made the universe."

These verses in Hebrews point to the culmination of biblical revelation in the eternal Son of God. This Son became incarnate in Jesus of Nazareth, forever uniting God and man in one person—100 percent God and 100 percent man (John 1:14). The prophecies, promises, longings, and anticipations under the old covenant find their fulfillment, meaning, and culmination in the life, death, and resurrection of Jesus Christ. As the apostle Paul says in 2 Corinthians 1:20, "For no matter how many promises God has made, they are 'Yes' in Christ."

The purpose of the Bible, then, is "to make [a person] wise for salvation through faith in Christ Jesus" (2 Tim. 3:15). The Bible is not an end in itself. As Jesus said to the religious experts in his day, "You diligently study the Scriptures because you think that by them you possess eternal life. These are the Scriptures that testify about me" (John 5:39). So, under divine superintendence, the goal of the Bible is to bring its readers to receive the forgiveness of God in Christ and thus to possession of eternal life in relationship with the triune God (John 17:3).

Basic Story Line of the Bible

The Bible explains the origin of the universe (God made everything, Gen. 1–2). The Bible also reveals why there is sin, disease, and death (humans rebelled against God and brought sin and decay into the world, Gen. 3:1–24). And, the Bible promises that God will send a

Messiah (Jesus) who will defeat death and Satan and ultimately renew all things (Gen. 3:15; Rev. 22:1–5).

God prepared for the coming of this Messiah by focusing his revelatory and saving work on the descendants of Abraham—that is, the Israelites or the Jews. Even as God gave his holy laws and sent his prophets to the one nation Israel, it was clear that he planned a worldwide blessing flowing forth from the Jews at a future time. God promised Abraham, "*All peoples* on earth will be blessed through you" (Gen. 12:3, my emphasis). Likewise, in the book of Isaiah, we read of God speaking prophetically to the coming Messiah: "It is too small a thing for you to be my servant to restore the tribes of Jacob and bring back those of Israel I have kept. *I will also make you a light for the Gentiles, that you may bring my salvation to the ends of the earth*" (Isa. 49:6, my emphasis). According to the Bible, Jesus has now inaugurated this worldwide salvation, which will be consummated at his return. While all persons are justly condemned under God's holy wrath, Jesus' death on the cross provides forgiveness for those who trust in him. A person becomes a part of God's people—a subject of King Jesus' domain—by turning away from his rebellion and trusting in the Savior's substitutionary death for his sin. As we read in John 3:36, "Whoever believes in the Son has eternal life, but whoever rejects the Son will not see life, for God's wrath remains on him."

The consummation of God's salvation is yet to be revealed. The Bible teaches that Jesus certainly will come again (1 Thess. 4:13–18). While scholars debate some of the specifics concerning Jesus' return, the Scriptures are clear that death and sin (now already defeated by the cross) then will be done away with forever (Rev. 20:14–21:4). All who have received God's forgiveness in Christ will dwell with God forever in endless joy (John 14:2–3; 17:24). Those who have remained in rebellion against God will not be given a postmortem, second chance at repentance; they will be punished through eternal separation from God (John 3:36; Matt. 25:46).

Functions of the Bible

Under the overarching purpose of revealing God and bringing people into a saving relationship with him through Jesus Christ, there are a number of related functions of the Bible, including the following.

- *Conviction of Sin.* The Holy Spirit applies God's Word to the human heart, convicting people of having failed to meet God's holy standard and convincing them of their just condemnation and need for a Savior (Rom. 3:20; Gal. 3:22–25; Heb. 4:12–13).

- *Correction and Instruction.* The Bible corrects and instructs God's people, teaching them who God is, who they are, and what God expects of them. Both through a believer's individual study and through the church's gifted teachers, God edifies and corrects his people (Josh. 1:8; Ps. 119:98–99; Matt. 7:24–27; 1 Cor. 10:11; Eph. 4:11–12; 2 Tim. 3:16; 4:1–4).

- *Spiritual Fruitfulness.* As the Word of God takes deep root in true believers, it produces a harvest of righteousness—a genuine manifestation of love for God and love for others (Mark 4:1–20; James 1:22–25).

- *Perseverance.* Empowered by the Holy Spirit, believers hold fast to the saving message of the Scriptures through the trials and temptations of life. Through this perseverance, they gain increasing confidence in God's promise to keep them until the end (John 10:28–29; 1 Cor. 15:2; 2 Cor. 13:5; Gal. 3:1–5; Phil. 1:6; Col. 1:23; 1 Tim. 3:13; 1 John 2:14).

- *Joy and Delight.* To those who know God, the Bible is a source of unending joy and delight. As Psalm 19:9–10 attests, "The ordinances of the LORD are sure and altogether righteous. They are more precious than gold, than much pure gold; they are sweeter than honey, than honey from the comb."

- *Ultimate Authority in Doctrine and Deed.* The Bible is the ultimate authority for the Christian in terms of behavior and belief (Luke 10:26; 24:44–45; John 10:35; 2 Tim. 3:16; 4:1–4; 2 Peter 3:16). The correctness of all preaching, creeds, doctrines, or opinions is decisively settled by this question: What does the Bible say? As John Stott notes, "Scripture is the royal scepter by which King Jesus governs his church."[1]

---

1. John R. W. Stott, *John Stott on the Bible and the Christian Life: Six Sessions on the Authority, Interpretation, and Use of Scripture* (Grand Rapids: Zondervan, 2006). The quote is from the first DVD lecture, "The Authority of Scripture."

Chronology of the Bible's Composition

The first five books in the Old Testament, the books of Moses (Genesis, Exodus, Leviticus, Numbers, Deuteronomy), most likely were written around 1400 B.C.[2] As the books describe events from thousands of years prior, however, it is almost certain that many oral and written sources underlie our current text. Of course, Moses' selection or editing of such sources took place under God's superintendence. The last book in the Old Testament, Malachi, was written around 430 B.C. So, the thirty-nine books of the Old Testament were composed over a thousand-year span by about forty different authors. (Some books in the Old Testament were written by the same author—Jeremiah and Lamentations, for example. Other books, such as 1 and 2 Kings, do not explicitly cite an author. Still other books, such as the Psalms or Proverbs, cite multiple authors for various portions.) The Old Testament was written in Hebrew with a few small portions in Aramaic (Ezra 4:8–6:18; 7:12–26; Dan. 2:4b–7:28; Jer. 10:11).[3]

The first book of the New Testament (possibly James or Galatians) likely was written in A.D. mid to late 40s. Most of the books in the New Testament were written in the 50s and 60s. The last book of the New Testament, the book of Revelation, also called the Apocalypse of John, probably was written around A.D. 90. The New Testament was written in Greek, the *lingua franca* of its day, though it contains a few transliterated Aramaic and Latin words.

Figure 1 provides a brief outline of the Bible's major events.

FIGURE 1: TIME LINE OF BIBLICAL EVENTS AND BOOKS	
Adam and Eve	*l.t.a.*[4]
Noah	*l.t.a.*
The calling of Abraham	2000 B.C.

(cont.)

---

2. Some scholars think Job predates the books of Moses.
3. Also, two words in Genesis 31:47 are in Aramaic—*Jegar-sahadutha* ("heap of witness").
4. *L.t.a.* stands for "long time ago." While I believe that Adam and Eve were historical persons, I will not venture to guess the year that God created them. It was (we can all agree) a long time ago.

FIGURE 1 continued	
The exodus	1446 B.C. (first books of the Bible written by Moses)
The monarchy begins	1050 B.C. (God chooses Saul)
King David	1010–970 B.C.
King Solomon	970–930 B.C.
The divided kingdom	931 B.C. (Israel and Judah divided)
The Assyrian exile	722 B.C. (destruction of Samaria)
The Babylonian exile	586 B.C. (destruction of Jerusalem)
The Persian period	537 B.C. (return of Jews under Cyrus)
Second temple finished	515 B.C.
Nehemiah/Ezra	mid-400s B.C.
Malachi (last Old Testament book)	430 B.C.
Intertestamental period	430 B.C.–A.D. 45
Jesus' birth	7–4 B.C.
Jesus' ministry	A.D. 27–30
Jesus' crucifixion	A.D. 30
First New Testament book(s) written	A.D. 45
Revelation written	A.D. 90 (last book of the New Testament)

REFLECTION QUESTIONS

1. What is one new thing that you learned about the Bible? (Or, possibly note a previously known fact that struck you afresh.)

2. One purpose of the Bible is to bring people into a saving relationship with God through Jesus Christ. Has that purpose been accomplished in your life? How do you know?

3. How would you rank your knowledge of the Bible on a scale of 1 to 10? How did you learn about the Bible? (Or, why do you not know much about the Bible?)

4. Have you read the entire Bible? If not, consider committing to do so over the next year.

5. Do you have a general question about the Bible that this section failed to answer? What is it?

FOR FURTHER STUDY

The Bible. (There is no better way to learn about the Bible than to read it for yourself. See chapter 7 for suggestions of which English translation to read.)

Carson, D. A. *For the Love of God: A Daily Companion for Discovering the Riches of God's Word.* Vols. 1 and 2. Wheaton, IL: Crossway, 1998, 1999. (These devotional books include one-page readings for each day and a Bible-reading plan that takes you through the Old Testament once and the New Testament twice in one year. Carson's writing is faithful and insightful, though challenging for persons with little biblical knowledge.)

CHAPTER 2

The Organization of the Bible

Maybe you grew up in a church where the children participated in competitions to memorize the locations of the books in the Bible. Or perhaps you are unsure of the order of the books of the Bible and feel intimidated when asked to look up a verse. Is there any discernible order or logic in the way the books in the Bible are arranged? When were chapter and verse divisions added? These are some of the questions we will answer below.

The Basic Division—The Testaments

The first three-fourths of the Bible was written between 1400 B.C. and 430 B.C. It includes thirty-nine books in the Hebrew language (Daniel and Ezra have a few small portions in Aramaic, a related Semitic language).[1] This part of the Bible is called the Old Testament. Non-Christian Jews, of course, simply refer to these books as their Scripture, or TANAK (Hebrew acrostic for Law, Prophets, and Writings). Jews who reject Jesus as Messiah do not recognize the New Testament as inspired.

The word *testament* comes from the Latin word *testamentum*, meaning "covenant" or "agreement." Apparently the first person to use this term to describe the divisions of the Bible was the early Christian apologist Tertullian (A.D. 160–225).[2] The idea of the Bible being organized around two covenants between God and humanity was not new to Tertullian, however, but is found explicitly in several biblical texts.

Jeremiah 31:31–33, written between 626 and 580 B.C., predicts the coming of the Messiah with explicit reference to a new covenant.

---

1. Jeremiah 10:11 is also in Aramaic, as are two words in Genesis 31:47, *Jegar-sahadutha* ("heap of witness").
2. *Against Marcion* 3.14; 4.6.

"The time is coming," declares the LORD, "when I will make a *new covenant* with the house of Israel and with the house of Judah. It will not be like the *covenant* I made with their forefathers when I took them by the hand to lead them out of Egypt, because they broke my *covenant*, though I was a husband to them," declares the LORD. "This is the *covenant* I will make with the house of Israel after that time," declares the LORD. "I will put my law in their minds and write it on their hearts. I will be their God, and they will be my people." (my emphasis)

In instituting the Lord's Supper on the night he was betrayed, Jesus alluded to the fulfillment of Jeremiah's prophecy in his death, saying, "This cup is the *new covenant* in my blood, which is poured out for you" (Luke 22:20, my emphasis). Because Jesus taught that his death and resurrection instituted God's promised new covenant, it was only natural for books that witnessed to and expounded on this reality to be referred to as the New Testament. Thus, Christians call the twenty-seven inspired books that came from Jesus' apostles and their companions the New Testament. These books, which make up the latter one-fourth of the Bible, were written between A.D. 45 and 90.

Number and Order of the Old Testament Books

The Old Testament includes thirty-nine individual books. These books vary in literary genre from historical narrative to romantic poetry. As they stand currently in our English Bible, they are organized somewhat topically (see figure 2).

- *Law (Genesis–Deuteronomy).* These five books are also called the Books of Moses or the Pentateuch. (*Pentateuch* is a Greek word meaning "the five books.") These books describe the origin of the world, the beginnings of the nation of Israel, God's choosing of Israel, the giving of his laws to them, and his bringing them to the border of the Promised Land.

- *The Historical Books (Joshua–Esther).* These twelve books recount God's dealings with Israel, primarily through historical narrative.

- *Wisdom and Songs (Job–Song of Solomon).* These five books include proverbs, other ancient wisdom literature, and songs.

- *The Major Prophets (Isaiah–Daniel).* These five books are called the major prophets because they are longer, not because they are more important. These books witness to God's many warnings, instructions, and promises that he sent to Israel through his divine spokesmen, the prophets.

- *The Minor Prophets (Hosea–Malachi).* These prophetic books are shorter and are thus called the minor ones. In the ancient Jewish collection of Scriptures, they were counted as one book, called The Book of the Twelve (that is, the twelve prophetic books).

FIGURE 2: THE OLD TESTAMENT

LAW	HISTORICAL BOOKS	WISDOM BOOKS	PROPHETICAL BOOKS
			MAJOR PROPHETS
Genesis	Joshua	Job	Isaiah
Exodus	Judges	Psalms	Jeremiah
Leviticus	Ruth	Proverbs	Lamentations
Numbers	1–2 Samuel	Ecclesiastes	Ezekiel
Deuteronomy	1–2 Kings	Song of Solomon (Song of Songs)	Daniel
	1–2 Chronicles		MINOR PROPHETS
	Ezra		Hosea—Malachi (The Twelve)
	Nehemiah		
	Esther		

If one were to visit a modern-day Jewish synagogue ("temple") and pick up a copy of the Hebrew Scriptures, it would include exactly the same contents as the Christian Old Testament but in a different arrangement. From ancient times, the Jews have organized their holy writings in three main divisions—Law (*Torah*), Prophets (*Nebi'im*), and Writings (*Kethubim*). The first five books of the Hebrew Bible are the same as the Christian Old Testament—the books of Moses, or the Law. After that, however, the order changes noticeably, and sometimes multiple books are grouped together. The last book in the Hebrew Bible is 2 Chronicles.

Jesus possibly alludes to the traditional Jewish order of the Hebrew Scriptures in Luke 11:49–51, where he says,

> Because of this, God in his wisdom said, "I will send them prophets and apostles, some of whom they will kill and others they will per- secute." Therefore this generation will be held responsible for the blood of all the prophets that has been shed since the beginning of the world, from the blood of Abel to the blood of Zechariah, who was killed between the altar and the sanctuary. Yes, I tell you, this generation will be held responsible for it all.

According to the Jewish canonical order, the Hebrew Bible begins with Genesis and ends with 2 Chronicles. Thus, Abel is the first martyr (Gen. 4:8), and Zechariah is the last (2 Chron. 24:20–22). Jesus also references the threefold division of the Jewish canon when he speaks of "the Law of Moses, the Prophets and the Psalms" (Luke 24:44). (Sometimes the Writings section was simply referred to with the most prominently used book in that section—the Psalms.)[3] When the Hebrew Bible was translated into Greek and Latin, the books began to appear in a more topical arrangement, from which we ultimately derive our order in the English Bible. Even so, there is not complete unifor- mity of book order among early Greek and Latin manuscripts or later translations. Knowing of this variety in the manuscripts should prevent modern interpreters from claiming divine sanction or meaning for any particular order of books in our current English Bible.

---

3. Paul D. Wegner notes that even in the tenth century, Arab historian al-Masudi re- fers to the Jewish canon as "the Law, the Prophets, and the Psalms, which are the 24 books" (*The Journey from Texts to Translations: The Origin and Development of the Bible* [Grand Rapids: Baker, 1999], 109).

Number and Order of the New Testament Books

During Jesus' earthly ministry, he used a variety of striking mnemonic devices (e.g., rhyme, unexpected details, and captivating stories). Furthermore, he promised his disciples that the Holy Spirit would bring his teaching to their memory (John 14:26). Following Jesus' resurrection and ascension, the stories of Jesus apparently were told for some time primarily as oral tradition that was carefully safeguarded and transmitted by eyewitnesses (Luke 1:1–4). Over time, authoritative collections of these stories were written and recognized by the church as having apostolic sanction—the four Gospels: Matthew, Mark, Luke, and John. Luke also wrote a second volume, Acts, explaining how the Holy Spirit came as predicted and propelled the early church outwards to testify about Jesus the Messiah.

As the apostles started churches all over the ancient Roman Empire, they continued instructing those communities through letters. From the earliest time, these apostolic letters were copied, circulated, and recognized as timelessly authoritative for the life of the church (Col. 4:16; 2 Peter 3:15–16). Thirteen of the letters in the New Testament were written by the apostle Paul (Romans–Philemon). Paul's letters are organized in the New Testament by decreasing order of size, first to communities and then to individuals.[4] If more than one letter was written to the same community or individual, the letters are kept together. The anonymous letter "to the Hebrews" (i.e., to Jewish Christians) was apparently included after Paul's letters because some people in the early church believed Paul or a Pauline companion wrote the letter.

Other New Testament letters were written by James, Peter, John, and Jude. Perhaps these letters are arranged in a decreasing order of prominence of the authors. Paul mentions "James, Cephas [Peter], and John" as Jerusalem church "pillars" in Galatians 2:9. This Pauline list mirrors the order of their respective letters in the New Testament (James, 1 Peter, 2 Peter, 1 John, 2 John, 3 John). The letter of Jude, a half-brother of Jesus, appears next. The final book of the New

---

4. One exception is Galatians, which, although it is slightly shorter than Ephesians, "may have been placed before Ephesians as a frontispiece to the collection of the Prison Epistles (Ephesians, Philippians, Colossians) because of its use of the term *kanōn* or 'rule' (Gal 6:16)" (William W. Klein, Craig L. Blomberg, and Robert L. Hubbard, *Introduction to Biblical Interpretation*, rev. ed. [Nashville: Thomas Nelson, 2004], 114).

Testament, the Revelation or Apocalypse of John, is a mixed genre, including letters, prophecy, and apocalypse. As much of the book is made up of visions and symbolic images that point to the end of the world, it is fitting as the last book of the twenty-seven-book New Testament canon (see figure 3).

It is worth noting that the practice of including multiple literary works within one book is not widely attested until at least the second century A.D. Prior to this time, most books in the Bible would have circulated as individual scrolls. A community of believers likely would have had a cabinet in which they kept the various scrolls with tags on the end to identify their contents. In the second and third century, however, books with multiple leaves (i.e., codices) began to appear with greater frequency. Some scholars have suggested that the canonical impulse of early Christians was the force behind the creation of the codex.

FIGURE 3: THE NEW TESTAMENT		
GOSPELS AND ACTS	PAULINE LETTERS	GENERAL LETTERS AND REVELATION
Matthew	Romans	Hebrews
Mark	1–2 Corinthians	James
Luke	Galatians	1–2 Peter
John	Ephesians	1–3 John
Acts	Philippians	Jude
	Colossians	Revelation
	1–2 Thessalonians	
	1–2 Timothy	
	Titus	
	Philemon	

Chapter Divisions

Early Christians and Jews often cited Scripture with reference to a book, author, or textual event but with little further specificity. Jesus, for example, in referencing the account of Moses, refers to the text simply with the phrase "at the bush [passage]" (Mark 12:26; Luke 20:37, my translation). As biblical texts came to be copied, read, and commented on, some made various attempts to further subdivide and label them. For example, Eusebius (ca. A.D. 260–340), a prominent historian in the early church, divided the four Gospels into a number of canons, or divisions. Eusebian canons are included in such ancient manuscripts as Codex Sinaiticus. Likewise, ancient Jewish rabbis applied various organizational subdivisions to the text.

Our current chapter divisions were added to the Old and New Testament by Stephen Langton (1150–1228), Archbishop of Canterbury in the early thirteenth century, while he was lecturing at the University of Paris.[5] Langton added the divisions to the Latin text, and subsequent publications came to follow his format. Langton's chapter divisions were inserted in modified form to the Hebrew text by Salomon ben Ishmael around A.D. 1330.[6] In light of this background, it seems unwise to claim any divine meaning behind Langton's chapter divisions, which are widely recognized to break the text unnaturally at some points. For example, the division between chapters 10 and 11 of 1 Corinthians introduces an unnatural split in Paul's thought.

Verse Divisions

Verse divisions in our modern English Old Testament are based on the versification standardized by the Ben Asher family (Jewish scribes) around A.D. 900. When Langton's chapter divisions were added to the Hebrew Bible at a later date (see above), the chapter divisions were sometimes adjusted to fit the Ben Asher scheme.[7] Thus, there are sometimes slight differences between the chapter and verse numbers of Hebrew and English Bibles. Scholars generally recognize the superiority of the Hebrew divisions in keeping together thought units.

---

5. Bruce M. Metzger, *Manuscripts of the Greek Bible: An Introduction to Palaeography* (New York: Oxford University Press, 1981), 41.
6. Wegner, *Journey from Texts to Translations*, 176.
7. Ibid.

Verse divisions in the New Testament were added to a Latin/ Greek diglot text in 1551 by Robert "Stephanus" Estienne, a printer from Paris. Drawing from an obscure comment by Estienne's son, some scholars have claimed that the printer made the verse divisions while riding horseback on a journey from Paris to Lyons (thus explaining the sometimes unnatural breaks). More likely, Estienne's son intended to say that his father divided the text while resting at inns during the trip.[8]

Prior to Estienne's verse divisions, biblical scholars were forced to refer to texts with phrases such as "halfway through chapter 4 in Galatians." However flawed, Estienne's versification was a major advance in allowing for specificity in citation. The first English Bible to have verse divisions was the Geneva Bible of 1560. Though Estienne is still criticized for some of his segmentations, it is virtually unthinkable that any other scheme will ever challenge the universal acceptance of his system. Again, knowing the history of our current verse divisions should prevent us from engaging in creative biblical mathematics, claiming divine meaning behind current verse numbers.

---

8. Metzger, *Manuscripts of the Greek Bible*, 41n.106.

REFLECTION QUESTIONS

1. When you have spoken of the Old Testament and New Testament, have you thought of the term *testament* as meaning "covenant"? How does viewing the Bible as based on covenants between God and humanity affect your reading?

2. Prior to reading the material above, where did you think the chapter and verse divisions in the Bible originated?

3. What is one new fact that you learned about the Bible in the section above?

4. Has this section raised any new questions for you?

5. Can you recite the Old Testament and New Testament books in order? If not, make it your goal to learn them over the next week.

FOR FURTHER STUDY

Patzia, Arthur G. *The Making of the New Testament: Origin, Collection, Text and Canon.* 2nd ed. Downers Grove, IL: InterVarsity Press, 2011.

Wegner, Paul D. *The Journey from Texts to Translations: The Origin and Development of the Bible.* Grand Rapids: Baker, 1999.

CHAPTER 3

The Authorship of the Bible

"God said it. I believe it. That settles it." So goes a popular fundamentalist mantra about the Bible. But if God wrote the Bible, why does Paul say in his letter to Philemon, "I, Paul, am writing this with my own hand" (Philem. 19)? Or, at the end of John's gospel, we read, "This is the disciple who testifies to these things and who wrote them down" (John 21:24). So, who did write the Bible—humans or God?

Theories of Inspiration

Everyone who claims the name "Christian" would agree that the Scriptures are inspired. Yet, a wide variety of meanings are attached to the adjective "inspired." What are some of the main theories of inspiration?

- *The Intuition Theory.* According to this view, the writers of the Bible exhibit a natural religious intuition that is also found in other great philosophical or religious thinkers, such as Confucius or Plato. Obviously, the absolute truth claims of Scripture are denied by those holding this view of inspiration.

- *The Illumination Theory.* This view holds that the Spirit of God in some way objectively impressed himself upon the consciousness of the biblical writers but not in a way that is essentially different from the way the Spirit communicates with all humanity. Only in degree is the Spirit's influence different, not in kind.

- *The Dynamic Theory.* This view asserts that God gave definite, specific impressions or concepts to the biblical authors but that he allowed the writers to communicate those concepts in their own words. That is, the exact phrasing of Scripture is due to human choice, while the main tenor of the content is determined by God.

- *The Dictation Theory.* This view holds that God dictated the exact words to the human authors. Like court stenographers, the authors of Scripture exercised no human volition in the composition of their writings. Sometimes those holding the verbal plenary theory (see below) are wrongly accused of believing in such mechanical dictation.

- *The Verbal Plenary Theory.* This view (the biblical one, I believe) asserts that there is a dual authorship to the Scriptures. While the authors of the Bible wrote as thinking, feeling human beings, God so mysteriously superintended the process that every word written was also the exact word he wanted to be written—free from all error. This view is sometimes called the verbal theory. It will be explored in greater detail in the following sections.[1]

The Dual Authorship of Scripture

When writing a letter to the Corinthians, Paul did not enter an ecstatic state, recite the letter to a secretary, and then, when finished, pick up the completed composition and say, "Let's see what God wrote!" Yet, as an apostle, Paul expected his teaching to be fully obeyed and believed—received, in fact, as the very word of God (1 Cor. 7:40; 14:36–37; 2 Cor. 2:17; 4:2; Col. 1:25; 1 Thess. 2:13; 2 Thess. 3:14). Similarly, Psalm 95 is clearly written by an ancient Israelite leading other ancient Israelites in worship. The psalm begins, "Come, let us sing for joy to the LORD; let us shout aloud to the Rock of our salvation. Let us come before him with thanksgiving and extol him with music and song" (Ps. 95:1–2). Yet, hundreds of years later, the author of Hebrews can quote Psalm 95 with the introductory citation, "The Holy Spirit says" (Heb. 3:7). Such apparent inconsistencies (Paul as author and his communication as the word of God; an ancient Israelite and the Holy Spirit as the author of the same psalm), in

---

1. This five-theory summary is derived from Millard J. Erickson, *Christian Theology*, 2nd ed. (Grand Rapids: Baker, 1998), 231–33. Erickson calls the verbal plenary theory the "verbal theory."

fact, convey a profound truth about Scripture—it is dually authored. Each word in the Bible is the word of a conscious human author and at the same time the exact word that God intends for the revelation of himself.

Variation within Dual Authorship

As is clear from a cursory glance at the Bible, God revealed himself "at many times and in various ways" (Heb. 1:1). Some Old Testament prophets gave oral denouncements, often with the repeated introductory phrase, "Thus says the Lord" (e.g., Isa. 7:7; Ezek. 2:4; Amos 1:3; Obad. 1:1; Mic. 2:3; Nah. 1:12; Hag. 1:5; Zech. 1:3; Mal. 1:4). Elsewhere, God's revelatory servants were given visions and prophecies, sometimes as the prophets themselves admitted their ignorance of all the meanings of their proclamations (Dan. 12:8–9; cf. 1 Peter 1:10–12). In other genres, the author's conscious role in composing or selecting the material is more on the surface of the text. For example, at the beginning of his gospel, Luke writes,

> Many have undertaken to draw up an account of the things that have been fulfilled among us, just as they were handed down to us by those who from the first were eyewitnesses and servants of the word. Therefore, since I myself have carefully investigated everything from the beginning, it seemed good also to me to write an orderly account for you, most excellent Theophilus, so that you may know the certainty of the things you have been taught. (Luke 1:1–4)

Note, Luke does not say, "I prayed and the Holy Spirit brought to my mind the stories of Jesus to write." Luke was a historian—engaged in real historical research. Yet, as an inspired companion of the apostles, Luke was also God's revelatory agent. Similarly, Paul's role in composing his own letters is undeniably on the surface of the text. For example, in Galatians 4:19–20, Paul is exasperated with the Galatians for their implicit denial of the gospel he preached to them. He writes, "My dear children, for whom I am again in the pains of childbirth until Christ is formed in you, how I wish I could be with you now and change my tone, because I am perplexed about you!" Undoubtedly, depending on the situation, authors were more or less conscious of relating divine revelation (for example, relaying a "Thus says the Lord" prophetic message versus the writing of a personal letter).

Much of the Bible comes as situational literature (documents addressed to specific persons facing particular historical situations), so it is worth asking how this situational literature can be the timeless Word of God. Muslims, for example, have in the Qur'an mostly abstract poetry that praises the attributes of Allah. Such poetry came to Mohammad, Muslims claim, in ecstatic utterance. The Bible, by contrast, testifies to God revealing himself in history through repeated, consistent, and anticipatory ways. That is, God spoke repeatedly to his people; he was consistent in his message; and, while God addressed the people in their current situation, his earlier revelation anticipates and points to a climactic intervention that ultimately came in Christ's life, death, and resurrection. Yet, it is not in abstract poetry but in the reality of daily life that God's Word came. Strikingly, when the Word of God became flesh (the incarnation), it was also in the seeming ordinariness of life that he appeared.

Some Implications of Dual Authorship

The fact that the Bible presents itself as a dually authored book has a number of implications for the way we approach it.

1. The clear purpose of the human author is a good place to start in understanding the Bible. The Scripture cannot mean *less* than the human authors consciously intended. Admittedly, there are a few places where the human author confesses his ignorance of the revelation given to him (e.g., Dan. 12:8–9), but these are exceptions. The human authors usually seem acutely aware of conveying timely messages to their current audiences.

2. God, as the Lord of history and revelation, included patterns or foreshadowing of which the human authors were not fully aware. Under God's sovereign hand, his prior historical interventions were in themselves prophetic—pointing forward to Christ. About the Old Testament regulations given to Israel, the author of Hebrews says, "The law is only a shadow of the good things that are coming—not the realities themselves" (Heb. 10:1). Similarly, Paul notes that the inclusion of the Gentiles and Jews together under the saving work of Christ was a "mystery" present in the Scriptures but not fully revealed until the Spirit declared this truth through the New

Testament prophets and apostles (Eph. 3:3–6). We should seek explicit statements in later revelation to clarify any such divine intentionality. One should be cautious about finding symbolic or prophetic details in the Old Testament when no New Testament author has provided authoritative interpretation of the text.

3. Sometimes it is asserted that the Bible can never mean something of which the human author was not consciously aware as he was writing. It is possible, however, to affirm a hermeneutical approach based on authorial intent without affirming the above statement. The biblical authors were conscious of being used by God to convey his word and believed that their revelation was part of a grand scheme of history. The Old Testament authors knew they were somewhere along the stair steps of revelation, but few, if any, knew how close they were to the top of the stairs (i.e., Christ). Though they could not know all the future events, the prophets certainly would not deny God's providential control of history, which exceeded their conscious reflection.

Inspiration and the Incarnation

It is often noted that the divine-human dual authorship of Scripture can be compared with the Lord Jesus Christ, who is both fully human and fully God. To some degree, this comparison can be helpful. Just as no one can explain exactly how both human and divine natures can be fully present in the one person of Jesus, neither can one explain fully how God so superintended the writing of Scripture so that each word is divinely inspired and yet also a word chosen by a human author. To affirm the divine and human natures of Christ and the divine-human authorship of Scripture, one need not be able to explain fully the mystery of these revealed truths.

T. C. Hammond's insightful comparison between inspiration and incarnation is worth quoting at length.

> The living Revelation was mysteriously brought into the world without the intervention of a human father. The Holy Spirit was the appointed Agent. The written revelation came into being by a similar process without the aid of human philosophical abstractions. The Holy Spirit was again the appointed Agent. The mother of our

Lord remained a human mother and her experiences throughout would appear to have been those of every other mother—except that she was made aware that her child was to be the long-expected Redeemer of Israel. The writers of the biblical books remained human authors, and their experiences appear to have been similarly natural, though they were sometimes aware that God was giving to the world through them a message of no ordinary importance (e.g., "For I received from the Lord what I also delivered to you . . ." 1 Cor. 11:23). Mary, the mother of our Lord, probably brought into the world other children by the normal process of birth. The writers of the biblical books probably wrote other purely personal letters which were not necessarily of canonical importance. More important still, no student should fail to grasp the fact that the divine-human personal life of our Lord is one and indivisible by any human means of analysis. On no recorded occasions can we say that in the one instance there was *purely divine* thought, and in the other a *purely human* thought. The two natures were united in one indissoluble Person. From the manger to the cross, the Lord must always be thought of and described from that point of view. Similarly, though the parallel is not quite complete, the student will be saved much unsound thinking, unnecessary confusion and, injury to his faith, by observing that in the Scriptures the divine and human elements are blended in such a way that in few cases can we, with any certainty, analyse the record to demonstrate purely human elements.[2]

One also should note that the divine-human dimension of the Bible concerns its authorship, *not* its very nature. We listen reverently to the Bible as the written Word of God, but we worship Jesus as the incarnate Son of God.

---

2. T. C. Hammond, *In Understanding Be Men: An Introductory Handbook of Christian Doctrine*, rev. and ed. David F. Wright, 6th ed. (Leicester: Inter-Varsity Press, 1968), 34–35. I have retained the author's nonstandard capitalization.

REFLECTION QUESTIONS

1. How can a letter from a dead man to dead people (Paul's letter to the Galatians, for example) be of significance to modern people?

2. Besides the Bible verses cited above, can you list other verses that point to the dual authorship of Scripture?

3. Is anything lost in ignoring or denying the human element in the writing of the Bible? Is it too simplistic to just say, "God wrote it"?

4. If one affirms the dual authorship of Scripture, what controls are left to prevent the finding of hidden "divine meanings" everywhere?

5. In what ways are Jesus' human and divine natures similar to and different from the divine-human authorship of Scripture?

FOR FURTHER STUDY

Carson, D. A. "Approaching the Bible." In *The New Bible Commentary: 21st Century Edition*, edited by D. A. Carson et al., 1–19. Downers Grove, IL: InterVarsity Press, 1994.

Erickson, Millard J. *Christian Theology*. 2nd ed. Grand Rapids: Baker, 1998. (See chap. 10, "The Preservation of Revelation: Inspiration," 224–45).

Marshall, I. Howard. *Biblical Inspiration*. Grand Rapids: Eerdmans, 1982. This book has been republished by Regent College Publishing.

CHAPTER 4

The Authority and Accuracy of the Bible

It is not uncommon to encounter people who assert that the Bible has errors in it. Such a view, however, does not square with the Bible's claims about itself or the historic view of the Christian church. What do we mean when the say the Bible is inerrant, and how can we support that assertion in light of alleged discrepancies in the Bible?

The Vocabulary of Inerrancy

Up until the mid-seventeenth century, essentially all persons who claimed the name of Christian accepted that the Bible was completely truthful in all matters that it asserted. With the elevation of human reason in the Enlightenment, however, some people began to have a more skeptical view of previously sacrosanct texts. People started to judge revelation (that is, the Bible) on the basis of their own human reason, rejecting and criticizing various portions, based on what seemed reasonable or probable to them. Many of these critics wanted to maintain some connection with the Christian church while at the same time making themselves the final arbiters of truth. Of course, the historic witness of the church to the complete truthfulness of Scripture has continued in spite of challenges, but the critics of it also have continued until this day.[1]

---

1. New challenges against inerrancy continue to appear. For a modern defense of inerrancy against recent detractors, see G. K. Beale, *The Erosion of Inerrancy in Evangelicalism: Responding to New Challenges to Biblical Authority* (Wheaton, IL: Crossway, 2008) and Norman L. Geisler and William C. Roach, *Defending Inerrancy: Affirming the Accuracy of Scripture for a New Generation* (Grand Rapids: Baker, 2011).

Within the last fifty years, due to increased Christian debates over the truthfulness of Scripture, a vocabulary has evolved to summarize various claims about the Bible's truthfulness. Below are some of the terms that are regularly used.

- *Inerrant/Inerrancy.* The doctrine of inerrancy, or the claim that the Scriptures are inerrant, means that the Bible is completely truthful in all things that the biblical authors assert—whether in geographic, chronological, or theological details. Advocates of inerrancy affirm a verbal plenary view of inspiration. That is, although the human authors of Scripture were thinking composers, God so superintended the writing process such that *every word* written was according to his will. The words were divinely guarded from all error. Wayne Grudem provides this helpful definition of inerrancy: "The inerrancy of Scripture means that Scripture in the original manuscripts does not affirm anything that is contrary to fact."[2] Similarly, Kenneth Kantzer writes, "Put quite simply, . . . inerrancy holds that the Bible tells us truth and never says what is not so."[3]

- *Infallible/Infallibility.* Infallible, according to modern dictionaries, also means "incapable of error."[4] However, the word has taken on more narrow connotations in current debates over the Bible. To claim the Scriptures as infallible is to assert that they are error-free *in* matters of theology or faith. This view is sometimes also called limited inerrancy. Advocates of full inerrancy certainly would affirm that the Scriptures are infallible, but not all persons who affirm the Bible's infallibility also would affirm full inerrancy. The word *infallible* is weaker in connotation and does not include within it the claim that the Bible is free from *all* error (intentional or unintentional, theological or non-theological). Those less familiar with the

---

2. Wayne Grudem, *Systematic Theology: An Introduction to Biblical Doctrine* (Grand Rapids: Zondervan; Leicester: Inter-Varsity Press, 1994), 90.

3. Kenneth S. Kantzer, foreword to *Encyclopedia of Bible Difficulties,* by Gleason L. Archer (Grand Rapids: Zondervan, 1982), 7.

4. This is the first definition of *infallible* in the Merriam-Webster Online Dictionary, www.merriam-webster.com (accessed November 14, 2012).

narrow connotations of the term *infallible* may unwittingly use it as a synonym for *inerrant*.

- *Inspired/Inspiration.* To claim the Bible as divinely inspired is to assert that God was somehow behind its writing. Without further clarification, this assertion is more ambiguous than the terms above. Some who claim the Bible as inspired also would maintain that non-biblical documents also are inspired or that God continues to inspire people in the same way today. Advocates of inerrancy claim that the Bible is inspired in a unique, verbal plenary way. See chapter 3 for a brief discussion of competing views of inspiration.

- *Neo-orthodox/Neo-orthodoxy.* *Neo-orthodoxy* literally means "new orthodoxy" and is a term used to describe a theological movement of the 1920s to the 1960s. Neo-orthodox scholars generally affirm that God revealed himself in history through mighty acts but that fallible human beings recorded these acts imperfectly. According to neo-orthodox theologians, these writings become the Word of God as they are newly proclaimed and people have an existential encounter with the living God. Though neo-orthodoxy is no longer a recognizable movement, the works of neo-orthodox theologians (e.g., Karl Barth, Emil Brunner) continue to exercise influence.

- *Trustworthy/True/Authoritative.* Sometimes critics charge that words like *inerrant* and *infallible* are not found in Scripture and wrongly focus on negation (that is, *no* error). Would it not be better, they ask, to use positive and historic terms such as *true, trustworthy,* or *authoritative*? While such positive affirmations admittedly are beneficial, modern debate over the Scripture has necessitated the precision of words such as *inerrant* (along with further explanatory comments on what *inerrant* means and does not mean). A glance at the history of Christian theology shows that new summary terms and qualifications often are required to combat theological error.

Scripture's Claims About Itself

Within the Bible itself, we find numerous claims and assumptions that the Scriptures are completely truthful in all that they assert (intentional or unintentional claims, theological or non-theological information). Below is a brief sampling of such Scriptures with a few explanatory comments.

- *Numbers 23:19*: *"God is not a man, that he should lie, nor a son of man, that he should change his mind. Does he speak and then not act? Does he promise and not fulfill?"* If God is completely truthful and the Bible is God's communication to humanity (Heb. 1:1–3), then it follows that the Bible, as God's Word, is completely truthful.

- *Psalm 12:6: "And the words of the* LORD *are flawless, like silver refined in a furnace of clay, purified seven times."* Psalms and Proverbs are filled with repeated praises of the perfections of God's Word. See especially Psalm 119.

- *2 Timothy 3:16: "All Scripture is God-breathed and is useful for teaching, rebuking, correcting and training in righteousness."* This verse asserts that while the Bible has human authors, the words they wrote must be attributed ultimately to the divine in-breathing (inspiration) of God.

- *2 Peter 1:21: "For prophecy never had its origin in the will of man, but men spoke from God as they were carried along by the Holy Spirit."* Again, this verse reminds us that each word written in the Bible is the exact word God intended to be written.

- *John 10:35: "The Scripture cannot be broken."* In his teachings and debates, Jesus repeatedly appealed to the Old Testament Scriptures, with the clear assumption that those texts were completely true in all they reported. Jesus referenced many persons and incidents of the Old Testament, assuming the factuality of all details. While Jesus frequently criticized distorted understandings of the Bible, he never questioned the veracity of the Scriptures themselves.[5] Like Jesus (as recorded in the Gospels), all the New Testament authors are unified in

---

5. See the definitive study by John Wenham, *Christ and the Bible*, 3rd ed. (Grand Rapids: Baker, 1994).

their citation of the Old Testament as a historically accurate work.[6]

- *Hebrews 1:1–2: "In the past God spoke to our forefathers through the prophets at many times and in various ways, but in these last days he has spoken to us by his Son, whom he appointed heir of all things, and through whom he made the universe."* If the prior anticipatory revelation of God (the Old Testament) was completely truthful ("God spoke"), how much more then should the culmination of God's revelation in Christ be received as completely trustworthy and authoritative.

The Historic View of the Christian Church

During the late nineteenth and twentieth centuries, the issue of the truthfulness of Scripture became a major dividing line between Christians in the United States. Denominations divided, and new denominations, schools, and mission agencies were founded as a result of this debate. Some non-inerrantists claimed that the so-called doctrine of inerrancy was really the creation of modern conservative Protestants, not the historic witness of the Christian church.[7] In response, overwhelming evidence has been presented to prove the contrary. While the exact term *inerrancy* (or non-English equivalents of this term) may not be found in early, medieval, or reformational church history, the *concept* or *idea* of inerrancy is the historic position of the church in all ages.[8] From 1977 to 1988, supporters of inerrancy worked through the International Council on Biblical Inerrancy and produced three formal, signed statements on inerrancy

---

6. See Grudem's list of references outside the four Gospels (*Systematic Theology*, 94).
7. See Jack B. Rogers and Donald K. McKim, *The Authority and Interpretation of the Bible: An Historical Approach* (San Francisco: Harper & Row, 1979); or, similarly, Russell H. Dilday, *The Doctrine of Biblical Authority* (Nashville: Convention Press, 1982), 57–59.
8. See John D. Woodbridge, *Biblical Authority: A Critique of the Rogers and McKim Proposal* (Grand Rapids: Zondervan, 1982). Erickson agrees: "The church throughout its history has believed in the freedom of the Bible from any untruths" (Millard J. Erickson, *Christian Theology*, 2nd ed. [Grand Rapids: Baker, 1998], 252). Also, see Article XVI of the Chicago Statement on Biblical Inerrancy: "We affirm that the doctrine of inerrancy has been integral to the Church's faith throughout its history. We deny that inerrancy is a doctrine invented by scholastic Protestantism, or is a reactionary position postulated in response to negative higher criticism."

and interpretation.[9] The most significant of these documents, the "Chicago Statement on Biblical Inerrancy" (1978), continues to serve as a touchstone for the definition of inerrancy.

Qualifications of Inerrancy

The doctrine of inerrancy must be properly explained and qualified to prevent misunderstanding. A number of important qualifications are listed below.

1. *Inerrancy applies only to the autographs (original copies of Scripture).*[10] No one denies that there are some copying errors in *every* Hebrew and Greek manuscript of the Bible (particularly with numbers, for example). Yet, with the vast number of Greek and Hebrew manuscripts and their careful transmission, we are able to reconstruct the original wording of the Old and New Testament with extreme accuracy.[11] For more detail on manuscript accuracy, see chapter 5.

---

9. According to a 1980 publication by the International Council on Biblical Inerrancy, "The International Council on Biblical Inerrancy is a California-based organization founded in 1977. It has as its purpose the defense and application of the doctrine of biblical inerrancy as an essential element for the authority of Scripture and a necessity for the health of the church. It was created to counter the drift from this important doctrinal foundation by significant segments of evangelicalism and the outright denial of it by other church movements" (from inside the front cover of R. C. Sproul, *Explaining Inerrancy: A Commentary*, ICBI Foundation Series, vol. 2 [Oakland, CA: International Council on Biblical Inerrancy, 1980]).

10. Article X of the Chicago Statement on Biblical Inerrancy reads: "We affirm that inspiration, strictly speaking, applies only to the autographic text of Scripture, which in the providence of God can be ascertained from available manuscripts with great accuracy. We further affirm that copies and translations of Scripture are the Word of God to the extent that they faithfully represent the original. We deny that any essential element of the Christian faith is affected by the absence of the autographs. We further deny that this absence renders the assertion of biblical inerrancy invalid or irrelevant."

11. Grudem writes, "For over 99 percent of the words of the Bible, we know what the original manuscript said" (*Systematic Theology*, 96). D. A. Carson says 96 to 97 percent of the New Testament's original wording is known with certainty ("Who Is This Jesus? Is He Risen?" a documentary film hosted by D. James Kennedy and Jerry Newcombe [Fort Lauderdale, FL: Coral Ridge Ministries, 2000]). No doctrinal issue is left in question by textual variations.

2. *Inerrancy respects the authorial intent of the passage and the literary conventions under which the author wrote.* If the author intended an assertion literally, we should understand it so. If the passage is figurative, likewise, we should interpret it accordingly. We must respect the level of precision intended, as well as the writing conventions of that day. For example, in Mark 1:2–3, Mark cites two different Old Testament texts (Isa. 40:3; Mal. 3:1) with the introductory phrase, "As it is written in Isaiah the prophet." Assuming our modern conventions of citation, this is an error because part of the quotation is from Malachi. But, as early Jews sometimes cited only one prophetic spokesman when quoting amalgamated texts, we should respect the literary conventions of Mark's day.[12]

3. As another example we can consider the order of events in the Synoptic Gospels. It is clear that the Gospel authors are not intending to give a strict chronological account of Jesus' ministry.[13] The material is frequently arranged topically. Thus, it should not surprise us to find a different order to Jesus' temptations in Luke 4:1–13 and Matthew 4:1–11. As the temple is a motif in Luke (e.g., Luke 1:9; 18:10; 23:45; 24:53; Acts 2:46; 5:20; 26:21), it appears that Luke has rearranged Jesus' temptations to place the pinnacle of the temple as the climactic temptation.[14] Or, possibly, as mountains are often of symbolic value in the gospel of Matthew (5:1; 8:1; 14:23; 15:29; 17:1; 28:16),

---

12. J. Marcus writes, "Such conflation of OT texts is familiar from postbiblical Judaism, especially from the Dead Sea Scrolls" (*Mark 1–8: A New Translation with Introduction and Commentary*, AB 27 [New York: Doubleday, 2000], 147).

13. Even Papias (ca. A.D. 70–155), notes, "And the elder [the apostle John?] used to say this: 'Mark, having become Peter's interpreter, wrote down accurately everything he remembered, though not in order, of the things either said or done by Christ. For he neither heard the Lord nor followed him, but afterward, as I said, followed Peter, who adapted his teachings as needed but had no intention of giving an ordered account of the Lord's sayings. Consequently Mark did nothing wrong in writing down some things as he remembered them, for he made it his one concern not to omit anything that he heard or to make any false statement in them'" (*Fragments of Papias* 3.15 in *The Apostolic Fathers: Greek Texts and English Translations*, ed. and trans. Michael W. Holmes, 3rd ed. [Grand Rapids: Baker, 2007], 739–41).

14. The word *temple* occurs forty-six times in Luke–Acts (NIV).

Matthew has done the rearranging. Part of faithful interpretation is respecting the individual emphases and purposes of the different authors and faithfully allowing those original emphases to come through in our teaching and preaching.

4. *Inerrancy allows for partial reporting, paraphrasing, and summarizing.* The words of a speaker, for example, might be summarized or paraphrased rather than given verbatim. As long as the meaning of the speaker is accurately conveyed, this reporting is completely truthful. Also, just as modern writers may choose to leave out certain details or emphasize other points, biblical writers did the same as they reported on the same events from different vantage points. For example, John reports more of Jesus' ministry in Jerusalem, while Matthew, Mark, and Luke focus on his itinerant Galilean ministry.

5. *Inerrancy allows for phenomenological language (that is, the description of phenomena as they are observed and experienced).* Humans often report events they see from their experiential vantage point rather than providing an objective scientific explanation. Thus, we would no more charge a biblical author with error when speaking of the sun rising (Ps. 19:6) than we would chastise a modern meteorologist for speaking of the anticipated time of tomorrow's sunrise. Neither the psalmist nor the meteorologist is intending to deny a heliocentric (sun-centered) solar system.

6. *Inerrancy allows the reporting of speech without the endorsement of the truthfulness of that speech (or the implication that everything else said by that person is truthful).* Psalm 14:1 says, "There is no God." Of course, in broader context, the passage reads, "The fool says in his heart, 'There is no God.'" Obviously, in reporting the speech of "the fool," the psalmist does not agree with him. Similarly, in quoting from pagan authors in his speech before the Athenians (Acts 17:22–31), Paul (and by extension, Luke, who records the speech) is not intending to endorse the truthfulness of everything written by Epimenides or Aratus (Acts 17:28).

7. *Inerrancy does not mean that the Bible provides definitive or exhaustive information on every topic.* No author in the Bible, for example, attempts a classification of mollusks or lessons in subatomic physics. The Bible tangentially touches on these subjects in asserting that God is the creator of all things, marine or subatomic, but one must not press the Scriptures to say more than they offer. If you want to learn how to bake French pastries, for example, there is no biblical text I can suggest. I can, however, exhort you to do all things diligently for God's glory (Col. 3:17) and not to engage in gluttony (Prov. 23:20). And I would be happy to sample any of the pastries you make.

8. *Inerrancy is not invalidated by colloquial or nonstandard grammar or spelling.* Spelling and grammar vary within various linguistic, cultural, geographical, and economic groups without impinging on the truthfulness of the actual communication. As Wayne Grudem notes, "An uneducated backwoodsman in some rural area may be the most trusted man in the country even though his grammar is poor, because he has earned a reputation for never telling a lie. Similarly, there are a few statements in Scripture (in the original languages) that are ungrammatical (according to standards of proper grammar at that time) but still inerrant because they are completely true. The issue is *truthfulness* of speech."[15]

Recommendations for Dealing with Difficult Texts in the Bible

Below are a few recommendations for dealing with alleged discrepancies in the Bible.

1. *Be sure that you are interacting with real texts.* Do not allow another person's uninformed skepticism to poison your own intellect.

2. *Approach the text in trust, not as a skeptic.* Investigating the truthfulness of Christianity is to be encouraged.[16] Christianity

---

15. Grudem, *Systematic Theology,* 92.
16. See, for example, Lee Strobel, *The Case for Faith: A Journalist Investigates the Toughest Objections to Christianity* (Grand Rapids: Zondervan, 2000); Craig A.

has nothing to fear from the facts. However, there comes a point when one realizes that the Bible is internally consistent and its claims are frequently confirmed by externally verifiable data (that is, by other ancient sources, archaeology, etc.). Just as in a healthy marriage one trusts his or her spouse and does not live in constant doubt or suspicion, likewise a Christian trusts the biblical text in areas that cannot be confirmed by external criteria. For example, we have no external records confirming the visit of the magi to Herod (Matt. 2:1–12). Yet the jealous, distrustful behavior of Herod the Great in the gospel of Matthew certainly agrees with extrabiblical accounts of his character (see Josephus, *Antiquities* 17.6.5).

3. *Pray about a difficult text.* God is a loving Father who cares for his children. Jesus taught,

> Ask and it will be given to you; seek and you will find; knock and the door will be opened to you. For everyone who asks receives; he who seeks finds; and to him who knocks, the door will be opened. Which of you, if his son asks for bread, will give him a stone? Or if he asks for a fish, will give him a snake? If you, then, though you are evil, know how to give good gifts to your children, how much more will your Father in heaven give good gifts to those who ask him! (Matt. 7:7–11).

4. *Keep in mind the "Qualifications of Inerrancy" when dealing with difficult texts (see above).* Don't demand that ancient writers conform to your expected standards (demanding perfectly parallel, verbatim quotations, for example).

5. *Seek counsel when dealing with difficult texts.* Tell a Christian friend, pastor, or professor about your question. Sometimes the serpent of apparent error is defanged in articulating one's

---

Evans, *Fabricating Jesus: How Modern Scholars Distort the Gospels* (Downers Grove, IL: InterVarsity Press, 2008); and J. P. Moreland, *Scaling the Secular City: A Defense of Christianity* (Grand Rapids: Baker, 1987).

question. Consult the best evangelical commentaries on the subject.[17]

6. *Be willing to set a text aside for further consideration rather than force harmonization.* Augustine (A.D. 354–430) speaks of his trusting and patient approach to the canonical Scriptures:

> I have learned to yield this respect and honour only to the canonical books of Scripture: of these alone do I most firmly believe that the authors were completely free from error. And if in these writings I am perplexed by anything which appears to me opposed to truth, I do not hesitate to suppose that either the [manuscript] is faulty, or the translator has not caught the meaning of what was said, or I myself have failed to understand it.[18]

---

17. For suggestions on the best commentaries, see Tremper Longman, *Old Testament Commentary Survey*, 4th ed. (Grand Rapids: Baker, 2007); and D. A. Carson, *New Testament Commentary Survey*, 6th ed. (Grand Rapids: Baker, 2007). Also, you can consult reference works such as Gleason L. Archer's *Encyclopedia of Bible Difficulties* or an evangelical study Bible, such as *The Zondervan NIV Study Bible,* ed. Kenneth Barker et al., rev. ed. (Grand Rapids: Zondervan, 2008); or *The ESV Study Bible* (Wheaton, IL: Crossway, 2008).
18. Augustine, *Letter* 82.3. Translation by J. G. Cunningham, *Nicene and Post-Nicene Fathers*, 1st series, ed. Philip Schaff, vol. 1, 350.

REFLECTION QUESTIONS

1. Has anyone ever presented you with an alleged error in the Bible as an argument as to why it is not true? What was your response?

2. What is the most puzzling text in the Bible to you?

3. Why do people disagree on their assessment of the Bible's truthfulness—some seeing it as the inerrant Word of God and others viewing it as an unreliable collection of contradictory documents?

4. If a neighbor were to tell you that he didn't believe the Bible because it is "full of errors," how would you respond?

5. Have you ever met an "ungodly inerrantist" (someone with a verbal affirmation of the Bible's truthfulness but otherwise ungodly behavior)? What does the Bible say about this situation?

FOR FURTHER STUDY

Archer, Gleason L. *New International Encyclopedia of Bible Difficulties.* Grand Rapids: Zondervan, 2001.

_____. *A Survey of Old Testament Introduction.* Rev. ed. Chicago: Moody Press, 1994.

Beale, G. K. *The Erosion of Inerrancy in Evangelicalism: Responding to New Challenges to Biblical Authority.* Wheaton, IL: Crossway, 2008.

Blomberg, Craig L. *Making Sense of the New Testament: Three Crucial Questions.* Grand Rapids: Baker, 2004.

Bruce, F. F. *The New Testament Documents: Are They Reliable?* 6th ed. Downers Grove, IL: InterVarsity Press; Grand Rapids: Eerdmans, 1981.

"The Chicago Statement on Biblical Inerrancy." International Council on Biblical Inerrancy. October 1978. This can be found at various online sources, including www.etsjets.org/files/documents /Chicago_Statement.pdf.

Geisler, Norman L., and Thomas Howe. *The Big Book of Bible Difficulties: Clear and Concise Answers from Genesis to Revelation.* Grand Rapids: Baker, 2008.

Geisler, Norman L., and William C. Roach. *Defending Inerrancy: Affirming the Accuracy of Scripture for a New Generation.* Grand Rapids: Baker, 2011.

Kaiser, Walter C., Jr., Peter H. Davids, F. F. Bruce, and Manfred T. Brauch. *Hard Sayings of the Bible.* Downers Grove, IL: InterVarsity Press, 1996.

Kitchen, K. A. *On the Reliability of the Old Testament.* Grand Rapids: Eerdmans, 2003.

Poythress, Vern S. *Inerrancy and the Gospels: A God-Centered Approach to the Challenges of Harmonization.* Wheaton, IL: Crossway, 2012.

_____. *Inerrancy and Worldview: Answering Modern Challenges to the Bible.* Wheaton, IL: Crossway, 2012.

CHAPTER 5

The Textual History of the Bible

When discussing the Bible with non-Christians, one might hear the objection: "Yes, the Bible reads that way *now*, but everyone knows that it has been changed."[1] Does this objection have any substance to it? How do we know that the Bible in our hands is a faithful transmission of the words that the inspired authors originally wrote?

Overview of Textual Issues

The Old Testament originally was written in Hebrew (with a few Aramaic portions) between 1400 and 430 B.C. The New Testament was written in Greek between A.D. 45 and 90. The original copies of ancient documents are called the autographs (or *autographa*). All autographs of biblical books have been lost or destroyed, though we have thousands of ancient copies. The process of comparing and studying these copies to reconstruct the wording of the originals is called textual criticism. Textual criticism began to flourish in sixteenth-century Europe for a number of reasons. First, the printing press had been introduced in the mid-fifteenth century, which allowed for multiple exact copies of the same book—ideal for the collation and comparison of variant manuscripts.[2] Second, there was a revival of learning

---

1. In fact, Muslim apologists explain Muhammad's apparent acceptance of the Old and New Testaments (Sūrah 3:3) by arguing that the biblical texts were subsequently corrupted. Of course, we have complete manuscripts of the Old and New Testament that predate Muhammad (ca. A.D. 570–632) by two centuries. Such manuscripts, while containing variants, are in fundamental agreement with the textual basis of modern Bible translations.
2. The first printed (with a printing press) Hebrew Old Testament appeared in 1488. The printed Greek New Testament produced under the auspices of Cardinal Ximenes (the Complutensian Polyglot) was completed in 1514. The first printed Greek New Testament to be published was the work of Erasmus in 1516. See Paul D. Wegner, *The Journey from Texts to Translations: The Origin and Development of the Bible* (Grand Rapids: Baker, 1999), 266–67.

in Europe, resulting in a great interest in ancient languages, cultures, and texts. Third, the Protestant Reformation and Catholic Counter-Reformation focused scholarly attention on the Bible.

The science of textual criticism continued to develop, reaching new heights with the discovery of many ancient manuscripts in the nineteenth and twentieth centuries. As with any science, the particulars of textual criticism are very complex. (For example, consider the archaeological, paleographic, and linguistic expertise needed to accurately date and decipher just one ancient manuscript.) At the same time, most scholars, both liberal and conservative, agree that text criticism has served to confirm the reliable transmission of the Old and New Testament manuscripts. A leading biblical scholar, D. A. Carson, notes that the New Testament autographs can be reconstructed with roughly 96–97 percent accuracy.[3] Furthermore, no text in question affects Christian doctrine. That is, all Christian doctrines are firmly established without appealing to debated texts. Most unsolved textual issues have little or no doctrinal significance.

Modern translations of the Bible (for example, English Standard Version, New International Version, New Living Translation, etc.) include footnotes of significant variants. For example, at the bottom of the page, one will notice comments such as "Some manuscripts say . . ." or "Most early manuscripts do not include . . ." By quickly skimming these footnotes, one can get a sense of what debated textual issues remain.

The Copying of Ancient Texts

Because our modern culture is so accustomed to technologically advanced methods of communication, we sometimes exhibit suspicion toward more ancient methods of literature production. Nevertheless, it should be noted that ancient Jewish rabbis and early

---

3. Carson says, "Almost all text critics will acknowledge that 96, even 97 percent, of the Greek New Testament is morally certain. It's just not in dispute" ("Who is This Jesus? Is He Risen?" a documentary film hosted by D. James Kennedy and Jerry Newcombe [Fort Lauderdale, FL: Coral Ridge Ministries, 2000]). Klein, Blomberg, and Hubbard make a similar assessment: "Estimates suggest between 97 and 99 percent of the original New Testament can be reconstructed from the existing manuscripts beyond any measure of reasonable doubt. The percentage for the Old Testament is lower, but at least 90 percent or more" (William W. Klein, Craig L. Blomberg, and Robert L. Hubbard, *Introduction to Biblical Interpretation*, rev. ed. [Nashville: Thomas Nelson, 2004], 122).

Christian scribes usually exercised great precision in the copying of biblical texts. Jewish scribes followed detailed systems for counting letters in manuscripts and checking for accidental variations.[4] Likewise, Christian scribes showed great caution, often having multiple correctors read through their copies to check for errors. Inevitably, all hand-copied manuscripts have some variations, but striking accuracy is evidenced in most ancient copies of our Old and New Testaments.

The Old Testament

In 1947, the first part of a cache of ancient Jewish documents was discovered in caves near the Dead Sea. According to one story, a young Arab goat herder investigated a cave after throwing a rock in and hearing a piece of pottery (a scroll jar) break. The documents discovered in these caves apparently belonged to a Jewish sect, the Essenes, who lived in a separatist community in the Judean desert near the Dead Sea. When the Essenes fled from the attacking Romans around A.D. 70, they left a treasure trove of manuscripts for modern-day text critics. In addition to many interesting sectarian documents and other extrabiblical literature, scholars have found portions of all Old Testament books except Esther and Nehemiah. These manuscripts have come to be called the Dead Sea Scrolls. The documents represent manuscripts and copies of manuscripts from roughly 250 B.C. to A.D. 50. Prior to the discovery of the Dead Sea Scrolls, the most significant extant Hebrew Old Testament manuscripts were the Leningrad Codex (A.D. 1008) and Aleppo Codex (ca. A.D. 900). The Dead Sea Scrolls pushed the Hebrew manuscript evidence back a millennium earlier.[5]

While not without some textual puzzles, the Dead Sea Scrolls have confirmed that the Hebrew books of the Bible were meticulously and faithfully copied. The Old Testament preserved in the Leningrad Codex (A.D. 1008) and Dead Sea Scrolls (250 B.C.–A.D. 50) is fundamentally the same Hebrew base text used for modern English translations today. Any significant text variations will be noted in the footnotes of modern translations, sometimes after the abbreviation "DSS" (Dead Sea Scrolls). Even when considering all known Old Testament manuscripts and variations, Shemaryahu Talmon of The

---

4. See Wegner, *Journey from Texts to Translations*, 167, 171–72.
5. We do, however, have many copies of the Septuagint (Greek translation of the Old Testament), which predate the Leningrad and Aleppo Codices by centuries.

Hebrew University of Jerusalem, avers, "It should . . . be stressed that these errors and textual divergences between the versions materially affect the intrinsic message only in relatively few instances."[6]

In addition to ancient Hebrew texts, we also have ancient copies of the Old Testament translated into several other languages—Greek, Latin, Syriac, etc. Ancient translations of the Old Testament sometimes can help in the deciphering of a difficult Hebrew word or phrase. More importantly, these texts sometimes can serve as helpful witnesses to variant readings in the ancient Hebrew (that is, they were translated from a Hebrew text that varied from the one we currently know). If translators suspect that an early translation may best preserve the original Hebrew wording, they may follow that wording in their English translation or footnote the variant. Again, see any pertinent Bible footnotes to see whether the Masoretic (Hebrew), Dead Sea Scrolls, Greek (Septuagint), or Syriac manuscripts are being followed. If your Bible lacks such notes, see the extensive translator footnotes for the free online NET Bible (New English Translation) at www.bible.org.

The New Testament

Even within the Bible itself, we find evidence of New Testament documents being hand-copied and circulated (Col. 4:16; 1 Thess. 5:27; 2 Peter 3:15–16). As these copies continued to increase and copies were made of copies, certain uniform scribal tendencies came to be embodied in various text families, usually classified according to geographic provenance—Western, Alexandrian, Byzantine, and Caesarean. The Greek-speaking Byzantine Empire was a region that continued to need and produce more Greek copies of the New Testament, so the Byzantine text family was copied the most. Yet most scholars agree that the Byzantine text family usually does not represent the oldest or most reliable reading.

By comparing ancient witnesses within the various text traditions, we can approach with amazing accuracy the wording of the autographs. In speaking of text families and manuscript variations, the unstudied reader can jump to wrong conclusions about the amount or significance of variations in the ancient manuscripts. Most

---

6. Shemaryahu Talmon, "The Old Testament Text," in *The Cambridge History of the Bible: From the Beginnings to Jerome*, ed. P. R. Ackroyd and C. F. Evans (Cambridge: Cambridge University Press, 1970), 1:162.

variations have little or no effect on the overall unified message of the New Testament. As a professor who teaches text criticism to intermediate-level Greek students, I have found that a detailed study of text criticism serves to increase students' trust in the Bible.

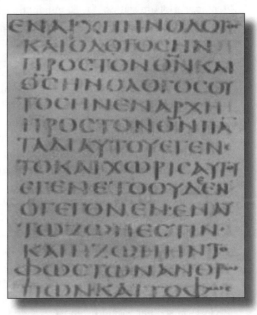

FIGURE 4: THE BEGINNING OF THE GOSPEL OF JOHN FROM CODEX SINAITICUS.

Codex Sinaiticus is a late fourth century manuscript. To view the entire manuscript, go to the following Web site: www.codexsinaiticus.org.

We have nearly six thousand ancient manuscripts or portions of manuscripts of the New Testament.[7] (For a photograph of one of the most famous manuscripts, see figure 4.) The oldest extant fragment of the New Testament comes from about A.D. 130.[8] No other ancient text comes even close to having this amount of early textual evidence. The classically trained F. F. Bruce once compared the textual evidence

---

7. The most recent count is more than 5,800 manuscripts, with the number increasing yearly (Daniel B. Wallace, private email correspondence, March 31, 2012). Wallace serves as executive director of The Center for the Study of New Testament Manuscripts (www.csntm.org).

8. The John Rylands fragment of John 18:31–33, 37–38. In February 2012, Daniel Wallace announced the discovery of seven new papyri that contain portions of the New Testament. One of these papyri contains a portion of the gospel of Mark and reportedly comes from the late first century. If this claim is confirmed, then the John Rylands fragment would no longer be the earliest extant portion of the New Testament. See www.csntm.org for more information.

for the New Testament to other well-known ancient Greco-Roman literature, noting:

> Perhaps we can appreciate how wealthy the New Testament is in manuscript attestation if we compare the textual material for other ancient historical works. For Caesar's *Gallic War* (composed between 58 and 50 B.C.) there are several extant MSS [manuscripts], but only nine or ten are good, and the oldest is some 900 years later than Caesar's day. Of the 142 books of the *Roman History* of Livy (59 B.C.–A.D. 17) only thirty-five survive; these are known to us from not more than twenty MSS of any consequence, only one of which, and that containing fragments of Books iii–vi, is as old as the fourth century. Of the fourteen books of the *Histories* of Tacitus (*c.* A.D. 100) only four and a half survive; of the sixteen books of his *Annals*, ten survive in full and two in part. The text of these extant portions of his two great historical works depends entirely on two MSS, one of the ninth century and one of the eleventh. The extant MSS of his minor works (*Dialogus de Oratoribus, Agricola, Germania*) all descend from a codex of the tenth century. The *History* of Thucydides (*c.* 460–400 B.C.) is known to us from eight MSS, the earliest belonging to *c.* A.D. 900, and a few papyrus scraps, belonging to about the beginning of the Christian era. The same is true of the *History* of Herodotus (*c.* 488–428 B.C.). Yet no classical scholar would listen to an argument that the authenticity of Herodotus or Thucydides is in doubt because the earliest MSS of their works which are of any use to us are over 1,300 years later than the originals.[9]

Samples of Textual Variants

To provide a better sense for the kind of variations that occur in ancient manuscripts, a few samples will be given below. The examples will be drawn from the New Testament, though similar examples could be given from the Old Testament.[10]

---

9. F. F. Bruce, *The New Testament Documents: Are They Reliable?*, 6th ed. (Downers Grove, IL: InterVarsity Press; Grand Rapids: Eerdmans, 1981), 16–17.
10. For a similar list of examples from the Old Testament, see Wegner, *Journey from Texts to Translations*, 180–81.

Unintentional Errors

According to one reckoning, 95 percent of textual variants are accidental—the unintentional variations introduced by tired or incompetent scribes.[11] Such variants include the following:[12]

1. *Errors of Sight.* Scribes sometimes copied texts by looking back and forth to the originals. By this method, they inevitably made a number of errors of sight. For example, they confused letters that looked similar in appearance, divided words wrongly (the oldest Greek manuscripts of the Bible have no spaces between words), repeated words or sections (that is, copied the same thing twice), accidentally skipped letters, words, or sections, or changed the order of letters in a word or words in a sentence.

2. *Errors of Hearing.* When scribes copied manuscripts through dictation (that is, scribes wrote as a manuscript was being read), errors of hearing were made. For example, vowels, diphthongs, or other sounds were misheard. (We make similar mistakes in English, for example, writing "night" when someone says "knight.")

3. *Errors of Writing.* Sometimes scribes introduced errors into texts simply by writing the wrong thing. For example, a scribe might accidentally add an additional letter to the end of a word, resulting in a different meaning.

4. *Errors of Judgment.* Sometimes scribes exercised poor judgment through incorporating marginal glosses (ancient footnotes) into the body of the text or similar unintentional corrupting influences.

Intentional Errors

The remaining 5 percent of textual variants resulted from intentional activity on the part of scribes. Such changes include:

---

11. Arthur G. Patzia, *The Making of the New Testament: Origin, Collection, Text and Canon*, 2nd ed. (Downers Grove, IL: InterVarsity Press, 2011), 230.
12. The material below is drawn from Patzia, *The Making of the New Testament*, 230–42.

1. *Revising Grammar and Spelling.* In an attempt to standardize grammar or spelling, scribes sometimes corrected what they perceived as orthographic or grammatical errors in the text they were copying.

2. *Harmonizing Similar Passages.* Scribes had a tendency to harmonize parallel passages and introduce uniformity to stylized expressions. For example, details from the same incident in multiple gospels might be included when copying any one gospel. As a professor of Greek, I have found it interesting that students sometimes unintentionally insert *Lord* or *Christ* when translating a passage with the name *Jesus*. Students, of course, are not intending to promote a higher Christology; they are simply conforming their speech to a stylized reference to the Savior. Ancient scribes behaved in a similar way.

3. *Eliminating Apparent Discrepancies and Difficulties.* Scribes sometimes fix what they perceived as a problem in the text. For example, in Mark 1:2-3, some manuscripts cite the amalgamated text as from "the prophets" rather than "Isaiah," as Mark wrote. See chapter 4 for a further discussion of this text and the issue of discrepancies.

4. *Conflating the Text.* Sometimes when a scribe knew of variant readings in the manuscript base from which he was copying, he would include both variants within his copy, conflating them together.

5. *Adapting Different Liturgical Traditions.* In a few isolated places, it is possible that church liturgy (that is, stylized prayers or praises) influenced some textual additions or wording changes (for example, Matthew 6:13b, "For yours is the kingdom, and the power, and the glory forever. Amen").

6. *Making Theological or Doctrinal Changes.* Sometimes scribes made theological or doctrinal changes—either omitting something they saw as wrong or making clarifying additions. For example, in Matthew 24:36, some manuscripts omit the

reference to the Son's ignorance of the day of his return—a passage that is obviously difficult to understand.[13]

Of course, with so many ancient texts at their disposal, text critics can dismiss most of the variants listed above, and therefore there is no need to cite the majority of variants in modern English translations. For the curious, more detailed discussions of manuscript variations can be found in reference works for text critics, critical editions of the Old and New Testaments, and scholarly commentaries.

Early Christian Orthodoxy and Other Ancient Manuscripts

Some sensationalistic writings have asserted that the Old and New Testaments show only the beliefs of those who won the doctrinal battles of ancient Judaism and early Christianity. In other words, there existed a plurality of competing religious views in ancient Judaism and early Christianity. As one view won out (monotheistic Judaism or orthodox Christianity), the winners rewrote history so that the losers never appeared to have a stake in the game. At a scholarly level, this view is represented by Walter Bauer's *Orthodoxy and Heresy in Earliest Christianity* (German original: 1934). On a popular level, this approach is embodied by the conspiracy-laden works of Dan Brown (*The Da Vinci Code*) and Bart Ehrman (*Misquoting Jesus*). Underlying such approaches is an extreme skepticism toward the Bible that will not hold up under more objective evaluation. A full-scale rebuttal of such aberrant views exceeds the parameters of this book, but for further study, the reader is referred to Darrell L. Bock's *The Missing Gospels* (in reply to Bauer or Brown), Timothy Paul Jones's *Misquoting Truth* (in reply to Ehrman's *Misquoting Jesus*), and Craig Evans's *Fabricating Jesus*.[14]

---

13. In this text, as in a few other places (e.g., John 4:6), Scripture seems to speak of Jesus from the perspective of his human nature, not intending to deny the omniscience or omnipotence of his divine nature. Others have explained this passage by claiming that prior to his exaltation, Jesus emptied himself of certain divine prerogatives (i.e., the kenotic theory).

14. Darrell L. Bock, *The Missing Gospels: Unearthing the Truth Behind Alternative Christianities* (Nashville: Thomas Nelson, 2006); Timothy Paul Jones, *Misquoting Truth: A Guide to the Fallacies of Bart Ehrman's Misquoting Jesus* (Downers Grove, IL: InterVarsity Press, 2007); and Craig A. Evans, *Fabricating Jesus: How Modern Scholars Distort the Gospels* (Downers Grove, IL: InterVarsity Press, 2008).

REFLECTION QUESTIONS

1. Before reading this chapter, had you ever considered the transmission of the ancient copies of our Old and New Testaments? If so, what prompted your interest?

2. When reading the Bible, do you look at the footnotes that deal with text variants? Why or why not?

3. What is something new that you learned about the transmission of biblical manuscripts?

4. Have you ever read a book by Bart Ehrman (*Misquoting Jesus*) or Dan Brown (*The Da Vinci Code*), or have you encountered other persons influenced by their works?

5. Do you have any remaining questions about textual variants or text criticism?

FOR FURTHER STUDY

Bock, Darrell L. *The Missing Gospels: Unearthing the Truth Behind Alternative Christianities*. Nashville: Thomas Nelson, 2006.

Bruce, F. F. *The New Testament Documents: Are They Reliable?* 6th ed. Downers Grove, IL: InterVarsity Press; Grand Rapids: Eerdmans, 1981.

Evans, Craig A. *Fabricating Jesus: How Modern Scholars Distort the Gospels*. Downers Grove, IL: InterVarsity Press, 2008.

Jones, Timothy Paul. *Misquoting Truth: A Guide to the Fallacies of Bart Ehrman's Misquoting Jesus*. Downers Grove, IL: InterVarsity Press, 2007.

Kaiser, Walter C. *The Old Testament Documents: Are They Reliable and Relevant?* Downers Grove, IL: InterVarsity Press, 2001.

Wegner, Paul D. *The Journey from Texts to Translations: The Origin and Development of the Bible*. Grand Rapids: Baker, 1999.

CHAPTER 6

The Canon of the Bible

The canon is the closed list of books that Christians view as uniquely authoritative and inspired. The Greek term *kanōn* originally meant "reed" or "measuring rod" and only later "norm" or "rule."[1] While the concept of a limited canon is ancient (Deut. 31:24–26; Dan. 9:2), the first person to use the Greek word *kanōn* to refer to Christianity's restricted list of inspired books was apparently Athanasius, bishop of Alexandria (ca. A.D. 352, *Decrees of the Synod of Nicea* 5.18).[2] The first church council to use the word *kanōn* in this way was the Synod of Laodicea (A.D. 363).[3] Very quickly, the term came to be widely used and accepted.[4]

For Protestant Christians, the canon is not an authorized collection of writings (in that the church conferred its authority or approval upon a list of books). Rather, the canon is a collection of authoritative writings. The biblical writings have an inherent authority as works uniquely inspired by God. Canonization is the process of recognizing that inherent authority, not bestowing it from an outside source.

Most Christians take the canon for granted without thinking about the process of the books' recognition. Oftentimes, only when a Christian encounters a person who rejects the canon outright (a non-Christian) or one who endorses a variation of the canon (a Roman Catholic who accepts the Apocrypha, for example) does he begin to think more

---

1. *Kanōn* is derived from the Hebrew word for reed or stalk, *qāneh*. See H. W. Beyer, "κανών," in *TDNT*, 3:596–602.
2. As cited in R. K. Harrison, *Introduction to the Old Testament* (Grand Rapids: Eerdmans, 1969; Peabody, MA: Prince [Hendrickson], 1999), 261.
3. While the synod's list of canonical New Testament books matches our own (except for the omission of Revelation), most scholars believe this list is a later addition (Bruce M. Metzger, *The Canon of the New Testament: Its Origin, Development, and Significance* [Oxford: Oxford University Press, 1987], 210).
4. David S. Dockery, *Christian Scripture: An Evangelical Perspective on Inspiration, Authority and Interpretation* (Nashville: Broadman & Holman, 1995), 89.

deeply about this issue. Who determined that thirty-nine books would be in the Old Testament canon and twenty-seven books in the New Testament canon? Why and when did they choose these books and not other books? Is the canon closed, or can additional books be added?

Old Testament Canon

The thirty-nine books in the Old Testament canon were written between roughly 1400 and 430 B.C. We do not have detailed information about the discussion that likely surrounded the inclusion or rejection of writings into the Old Testament. It seems that some books were recognized instantly as authoritative on the basis of their self-authenticating nature or a prophetic word being fulfilled (Exod. 24:3–7; Deut. 18:15–22; Dan. 9:2). Other books may have taken some time to be edited or fully recognized (Isa. 30:8; Prov. 25:1). Walter Kaiser summarizes the apparent history of the Old Testament canon: "[There was a] *progressive recognition* of certain books as being canonical right from their inception by readers and listeners who were contemporaries with the writers and who are thereby in the best position to determine the claims of the writers."[5] It seems clear that by the time of Jesus, most Jews were in agreement as to their own canon—a list that matches our current Old Testament in content.

The Samaritans (half-Jews) of Jesus' day recognized only an edited copy of the Pentateuch (the first five books of the Old Testament) as their Scripture, but Jews never viewed the Samaritans as legitimate descendants of Abraham (Matt. 10:5–6; Luke 17:18). A small but more mainstream Jewish party in Jesus' day, the Sadducees, viewed books outside the Pentateuch as less authoritative or inspired (Matt. 22:23; Acts 23:8). Jesus rejected the Sadducees' views, endorsing the threefold Jewish canon (Law, Prophets, Writings) as it stood in his day (Luke 24:44; note that the Psalms, as the largest of the Writings section, was sometimes used to refer to the whole section). For Christians, accepting the thirty-nine–book Old Testament canon is relatively easy. One might say, "Jesus and his apostles affirmed the Jewish canon of the Hebrew Scriptures in their day. As a follower of Jesus, I affirm the same."

In recent history, some Old Testament scholars have claimed that the Jewish canon was not closed until the so-called Jewish

---

5. Walter C. Kaiser Jr., *The Old Testament Documents: Are They Reliable and Relevant?* (Downers Grove, IL: InterVarsity Press, 2001), 31.

Council of Jamnia (or Jabneh) in A.D. 90.[6] The term *council* and a specific date are misleading, however. In actuality, following the destruction of the Jerusalem temple by the Romans in A.D. 70, rabbinic discussions continued on a variety of subjects in Jamnia for the next six decades.[7] Subsequent reexamination of the rabbinic discussion at Jamnia favors the traditional Christian view that the canon was long settled for the majority of Jews by the first century.[8] Jamnia provided a venue for the discussion of challenging Old Testament texts, but no binding canonical decisions were proclaimed.[9] Josephus claimed that the Jewish canon, which matches in content our modern Old Testament, had been settled from the time of the Persian King Artaxerxes (465–423 B.C.). The Jews in Josephus' and Jesus' day ordered their Hebrew Scriptures differently, resulting in twenty-four (or twenty-two) books, equaling our current number of thirty-nine books (see figure 5).[10] Josephus' statement

---

6. H. H. Graetz is apparently the originator of this idea (*Kohélet oder der Salominishe Prediger* [Leipzig: Winter, 1871], 160–63), followed by H. E. Ryle, *The Canon of the Old Testament* (London: Macmillan, 1892). More recently, see, for example, Bernhard Anderson, *Understanding the Old Testament*, 4th ed. (Englewood Cliffs, NJ: Prentice-Hall, 1986), 641. Liberal theories of canonical formation also date the books of the Old Testament much later.

7. Jack P. Lewis, "Jamnia (Jabneh), Council of," *The Anchor Bible Dictionary* 3:635–36.

8. Jack Lewis writes, "It would appear that the frequently made assertion that a binding decision was made at [Jamnia] covering all scripture is conjectural at best" ("What Do We Mean by Jabneh?" *Journal of Bible and Religion* 32 [1964]: 132). According to Sid Leiman, "The widespread view that the Council of Jamnia closed the biblical canon, or that it canonized any books at all, is not supported by the evidence and need no longer be seriously maintained" ("The Canonization of Hebrew Scripture: The Talmudic and Midrashic Evidence," *Transactions of the Connecticut Academy of Arts and Sciences* 47 [Hamden, CT: Archon, 1976], 124).

9. Admittedly, a minority of Jews did question the appropriateness of some texts or books (e.g., Song of Songs, Ecclesiastes), but such questioning continued, and, in fact, continues even among some Jewish scholars today. Giving Jamnia the most credit it could merit, Bruce writes, "The books which [the participants at Jamnia] decided to acknowledge as canonical were already generally accepted, although questions had been raised about them. Those which they refused to admit had never been included. They did not expel from the canon any book which had previously been admitted. The Council of Jamnia, as J. S. Wright puts it, 'was the confirming of public opinion, not the forming of it'" (F. F. Bruce, *The Books and the Parchments*, rev. ed. [London: Marshall Pickering, 1991], 88–89).

10. Josephus counts Judges–Ruth as one book and Jeremiah–Lamentations as one book, reducing the total number to twenty-two books.

FIGURE 5: ORDERING OF HEBREW SCRIPTURES

JEWISH SCRIPTURE (24 BOOKS)	THE CHRISTIAN OLD TESTAMENT (39 BOOKS)	
LAW	**HISTORICAL BOOKS**	
Genesis Exodus Leviticus Numbers Deuteronomy	Genesis Exodus Leviticus Numbers Deuteronomy Joshua Judges	Ruth 1–2 Samuel 1–2 Kings 1–2 Chronicles Ezra Nehemiah Esther
FORMER PROPHETS	**WISDOM BOOKS**	
Joshua Judges Samuel Kings	Job Psalms Proverbs Ecclesiastes Song of Solomon (Song of Songs)	
LATTER PROPHETS		
Major Prophets		
Isaiah Jeremiah Ezekiel		
Minor Prophets		
The Book of the Twelve (Hosea–Malachi)		
WRITINGS	**PROPHETICAL BOOKS**	
Psalms Job Proverbs Ruth Song of Solomon (Song of Songs) Ecclesiastes Lamentations Esther Daniel Ezra–Nehemiah Chronicles	**Major Prophets** Isaiah Jeremiah Lamentations Ezekiel Daniel	
	Minor Prophets	
	Hosea—Malachi (The 12)	

on the closure of the Hebrew canon (see the text box on page 66) is particularly striking. It is difficult to see why we should dismiss his unambiguous claims in favor of tenuous modern reconstructions.

New Testament Canon

Compared with the Old Testament canon, we know much more about the formal recognition of the books in the New Testament. In discussing the canon, the early church insisted that recognized books be:

- *Apostolic:* written by or tied closely to an apostle (an authorized eyewitness of Jesus).

- *Catholic:* widely, if not universally, recognized by the churches. The word catholic means universal. Its use here should not be confused with the way the word is used to identify various strains of Christianity.

- *Orthodox:* not in contradiction to any recognized apostolic book or doctrine.

The first canonical list that matches exactly our twenty-seven–book New Testament is the list by Athanasius in his Easter letter (letter 39) of A.D. 367. Two early church councils (Hippo Regius, A.D. 393, and Carthage, A.D. 397) confirmed the twenty-seven–book list.

Though an oversimplification, T. C. Hammond presents a helpful summary of the recognition of the New Testament canon.

- The New Testament books were written during the period A.D. 45–100.

- They were collected and read in the churches from A.D. 100–200.

- They were carefully examined and compared with spurious writings from A.D. 200–300. Complete agreement was obtained during the period A.D. 300–400.[11]

---

11. T. C. Hammond, *In Understanding Be Men: An Introductory Handbook of Christian Doctrine*, rev. and ed. David F. Wright, 6th ed. (Leicester: Inter-Varsity Press, 1968), 29. Hammond puts the books of the New Testament as written

Josephus (A.D. 37–100), the non-Christian Jewish historian, wrote about the discussions on the Hebrew canon:

> For we have not an innumerable multitude of books among us, disagreeing from, and contradicting one another, [as the Greeks have], but only twenty-two books, which contain the records of all the past times; which are justly believed to be divine; and of them five belong to Moses, which contain his laws and the traditions of the origin of mankind till his death. This interval of time was little short of three thousand years; but as to the time from the death of Moses till the reign of Artaxerxes, king of Persia, who reigned after Xerxes, the prophets, who were after Moses, wrote down what was done in their times in thirteen books. The remaining four books contain hymns to God, and precepts for the conduct of human life. It is true, our history has been written since Artaxerxes very particularly, but has not been esteemed of the like authority with the former by our forefathers, because there has not been an exact succession of prophets since that time; and how firmly we have given credit to these books of our own nation, is evident by what we do; for, during so many ages as have already passed, no one has been so bold as either to add anything to them, to take anything from them, or to make any change in them; but it is natural to all Jews, immediately and from their very birth, to esteem these books to contain divine doctrines, and to persist in them, and, if occasion be, willingly to die for them. (*Against Apion* 1:38–42, Whiston's translation)

Sometimes students are troubled to discover that we do not have a canonical list of New Testament books that exactly matches our own until Athanasius' letter of A.D. 367. Several facts must be remembered, however. First, all the New Testament documents were viewed as authoritative and were circulating among the churches by A.D. 90 or 100 (Col. 4:16; 2 Peter 3:16). Second, from the earliest post-New Testament Christian writings (the Apostolic Fathers), it is clear that an implicit canon existed. By their frequency of citation, the Apostolic

---

between A.D. 50 and 100, so I have adjusted his scheme by five years here. Also, canonical debates continued longer in the East.

Fathers attribute unique authority to what came to be called the New Testament.[12] Third, in the absence of a unified ecclesiastical hierarchy and in a situation where documents were copied by hand, it is not surprising that we find churches debating what writings were truly apostolic. Eusebius (ca. A.D. 260–340) mentions three categories of books in his day—the universally confessed, the debated, and the spurious.[13] Fourth, one must keep in mind the large geographic distances between some early Christian communities, as well as the persecutions that made communication and gatherings of decision-making bodies virtually impossible until the conversion of the Roman emperor in the fourth century A.D.

The observation of Barker, Lane, and Michaels is fitting:

> The fact that substantially the whole church came to recognize the same 27 books as canonical is remarkable when it is remembered that the result was not contrived. All that the several churches throughout the Empire could do was to witness to their own experience with the documents and share whatever knowledge they might have about their origin and character. When consideration is given to the diversity in cultural backgrounds and in orientation to the essentials of the Christian faith within the churches, their common agreement about which books belonged to the New Testament serves to suggest that this final decision did not originate solely at the human level.[14]

Beyond the valid historical questions of canon formation, however, Christians approach the canon of the Bible with certain presuppositions. If God accurately preserved the prior revelation of himself in the Old Testament writings (as endorsed by Jesus), how likely is it that the culmination of that revelation—the person and teaching of his Son—would fail to be recorded and preserved (Heb. 1:1–2)? Indeed, Jesus promises his apostles the presence of the Holy Spirit in bringing his teaching accurately to their memory and conveying further necessary information to his followers (John 14:26).

---

12. John Barton writes, "The central importance of most of the writings that would come to form the New Testament is already established in the early second century" (*Holy Writings, Sacred Text: The Canon in Early Christianity* [Louisville, KY: Westminster John Knox, 1997], 64).
13. Eusebius, *Historia Ecclesiastica* 3.25.1–5.
14. Glenn W. Barker, William L. Lane, and J. Ramsey Michaels, *The New Testament Speaks* (New York: Harper & Row, 1969), 29.

The Apocrypha

Roman Catholic and Orthodox Christians (Eastern Orthodox, Russian Orthodox, Ethiopian Orthodox, etc.) have some additional books in their Old Testaments that Protestants do not consider Scripture[15] (see figure 6). Protestants refer to these books as the Apocrypha, though Roman Catholics call them the deuterocanonical books (literally, the "secondly canonical" books, because they were formally recognized as canonical at a later time—as opposed to the protocanonical, or "firstly canonical," books). These books were written by Jews in the roughly five-hundred-year period between the Old and New Testaments (430 B.C.–A.D. 45).

Protestants do not consider the Apocrypha as Scripture for a number of reasons.

1. The Jews who authored the books never accepted them into their canon. This is a weighty argument in that those who wrote and preserved these books put them in a different category from the recognized Hebrew Scriptures. Indeed, comments within the Apocrypha distinguish contemporary writers from the divinely inspired prophets, who had long been silent (1 Macc. 4:41–46; 9:27; 14:40).

2. The Apocrypha contains clear factual errors and, from the standpoint of Protestants, theological errors (such as praying for the dead, see 2 Macc. 12:43–45).[16]

3. The Roman Catholic Church did not officially recognize (with a church-wide council) the books in the Apocrypha as canonical until the Council of Trent in 1546.[17] In fact, Jerome (A.D. 340–420), the translator of the Vulgate (the official Roman Catholic Latin Bible for more than a millennium), claimed the books of the Apocrypha were edifying for Christians but were "not for the establishing of the authority

---

15. See Hans Peter Rüger, "The Extent of the Old Testament Canon," *The Bible Translator* 40 (1989): 301–8.

16. For examples of errors, see table 8.4 ("Inaccuracies in the Apocryphal Books") in Paul D. Wegner, *The Journey from Texts to Translations: The Origin and Development of the Bible* (Grand Rapids: Baker, 1999), 125.

17 Some early regional councils and regular liturgical use, however, affirmed the Apocrypha as Scripture.

FIGURE 6: THE CANON IN VARYING CHRISTIAN TRADITIONS

PROTESTANTISM	ROMAN CATHOLICISM	GREEK ORTHODOXY
OLD TESTAMENT	OLD TESTAMENT	OLD TESTAMENT
Pentateuch (Gen.—Deut.) Prophets <ul><li>Former (Josh.—Kings)</li><li>Latter Major (Isa., Jer., Ezek.) Minor (The Twelve)</li></ul> Writings	Pentateuch (Gen.—Deut.) Prophets <ul><li>Former (Josh.—Kings)</li><li>Latter Major (Isa., Jer., Ezek.) Minor (The Twelve)</li></ul> Writings	Pentateuch (Gen.—Deut.) Prophets <ul><li>Former (Josh.—Kings)</li><li>Latter Major (Isa., Jer., Ezek.) Minor (The Twelve)</li></ul> Writings
	APOCRYPHA	APOCRYPHA
	Tobit Judith Additions to Esther Wisdom of Solomon Ecclesiasticus (Sirach) Baruch (+ Letter of Jeremiah) Prayer of Azariah Susanna Bel and the Dragon 1 Maccabees 2 Maccabees	Tobit Judith Additions to Esther Wisdom of Solomon Ecclesiasticus (Sirach) Baruch (+ Letter of Jeremiah) Prayer of Azariah Susanna Bel and the Dragon 1 Maccabees 2 Maccabees 1 Esdras (or 3 Ezra) Prayer of Manasseh 3 Maccabees 4 Maccabees (appendix) Psalm 151
NEW TESTAMENT	NEW TESTAMENT	NEW TESTAMENT
Gospels Acts Paul (and Hebrews) General Epistles Revelation	Gospels Acts Paul (and Hebrews) General Epistles Revelation	Gospels Acts Paul (and Hebrews) General Epistles Revelation

of the doctrines of the church."[18] At the Council of Trent, Roman Catholics recognized the deuterocanonical books in reaction to Protestant leaders who called for a return to biblical Christianity, stripped of later accretions and distortions. Roman Catholics include the apocryphal books within their Old Testament canon, sometimes adding whole books and sometimes combining apocryphal portions with books Protestants recognize as canonical (for example, three additions to Daniel—The Prayer of Azariah, Susanna, and Bel and the Dragon). These additions and combinations result in a forty-six–book Old Testament canon for Roman Catholics.[19]

4. While there are some debatable allusions to the Apocrypha in the New Testament, New Testament authors nowhere cite the Apocrypha as Scripture (that is, with a formula such as "The Scripture says"). In contrast, almost every book in the Old Testament is cited as Scripture by New Testament authors.[20]

The Apocrypha is helpful for understanding the historical and cultural changes that lead up to the New Testament. For example, by reading 1 and 2 Maccabees, one can learn about the origins of the Feast of Dedication (mentioned in John 10:22). The Apocrypha also contains entertaining stories (for example, Tobit, which would make a great Disney movie, or Susanna or Bel and the Dragon, which read like detective stories). Other parts of the Apocrypha occasionally sound similar to the Psalms or Proverbs (e.g., Sirach). In fact, Protestants sometimes unwittingly sing hymns based upon apocryphal texts ("It Came Upon a Midnight Clear," based on Wisdom of Solomon 18:14–15, and "Now Thank We All Our God," based on Sirach 50:22–24). Still, it is clear that the leaders of the Protestant Reformation were wise to return the church to its earliest

---

18. Jerome, *Prologus Galeatus*, as cited in Gleason L. Archer, *A Survey of Old Testament Introduction*, rev. ed. (Chicago: Moody Press, 1994), 81n.8.

19. *Catechism of the Catholic Church* (Liguori, MO: Liguori Publications, 1994), 34.

20. Gleason Archer notes that every Old Testament book is quoted or alluded to in the New Testament except Ruth, Ezra, and Song of Songs (*A Survey of Old Testament Introduction*, 83n.16). Most Old Testament books are cited unambiguously as Scripture.

understanding of the Apocrypha as interesting, sometimes beneficial, but uninspired literature.[21]

Is the Canon Closed?

According to the early church's categories for canonicity (apostolic, catholic, orthodox—see above), it would be impossible to have any additions to the canon. For example, even if a genuine and orthodox letter of the apostle Paul were discovered, that letter would not have had widespread usage in the early church (that is, it could never claim catholicity). The canon of Scripture is closed.

---

21. At the time of the Protestant Reformation, Lutherans and Anglicans (as opposed to Calvinists and Anabaptists) were more open to seeing the Apocrypha as devotionally beneficial (Norman L. Geisler and Ralph E. MacKenzie, *Roman Catholics and Evangelicals: Agreements and Differences* [Grand Rapids: Baker, 1995], 157n. 1).

REFLECTION QUESTIONS

1. Prior to the reading above, had you ever investigated the canon? What prompted your interest in turning to this question?

2. Explain the difference between "an authorized collection of writings" and "a collection of authoritative writings." Is this an important distinction?

3. If a Roman Catholic neighbor were to ask you, "Why do you Protestants cut some books out of the Bible?" How would you reply?

4. Is it possible to be a Christian and yet have a wrong understanding of the canon (as say, an Ethiopian Orthodox person would)? Explain.

5. Does the survey of the canon above leave any questions unanswered for you?

FOR FURTHER STUDY

Archer, Gleason L. *A Survey of Old Testament Introduction*. Rev. ed. Chicago: Moody Press, 1994 (see chap. 5, "The Canon of the Old Testament," 75–88).

Bruce, F. F. *The Books and the Parchments*. Rev. ed. London: Marshall Pickering, 1991.

_____. *The Canon of Scripture*. Leicester and Downers Grove, IL: InterVarsity Press, 1988.

Carson, D. A., and Douglas J. Moo. *An Introduction to the New Testament*. 2nd ed. Grand Rapids: Zondervan, 2005 (see chap. 26, "The New Testament Canon," 726–43).

Geisler, Norman L., and Ralph E. MacKenzie. *Roman Catholics and Evangelicals: Agreements and Differences*. Grand Rapids: Baker, 1995 (see chaps. 9–10).

Harrison, R. K. *Introduction to the Old Testament*. Grand Rapids: Eerdmans, 1969; reprint, Peabody, MA: Prince (Hendrickson), 1999 (see part 4, section 4, "The Old Testament Canon," 260–88).

Kruger, Michael J. *Canon Revisited: Establishing the Origins and Authority of the New Testament Books*. Wheaton, IL: Crossway, 2012.

Wegner, Paul D. *The Journey from Texts to Translations: The Origin and Development of the Bible*. Grand Rapids: Baker, 1999 (see pp. 101–51).

CHAPTER 7

Modern Translations of the Bible

When people discover that I am a New Testament professor, they often have religious questions they would like to ask. One of the most common is this: What English version of the Bible do you recommend? During the birth of my oldest daughter, the attending physician even asked me this question in the midst of my wife's labor! Alas, I received no medical discount for my advice.

The Original Languages of the Bible

The Bible was originally written in three different languages over a period of nearly fifteen hundred years (roughly 1400 B.C.–A.D. 90). The Old Testament was written in Hebrew, with a few Aramaic portions. The New Testament was written in Greek. While sections of the Old Testament previously had been translated into a few other languages (mainly Greek), as soon as the Christian gospel began to permeate other cultures, the entire Bible was quickly translated into many other languages—Syriac, Coptic, Ethiopic, Latin, etc.

History of the English Language

Any living language is constantly changing. Modern English (as classified by linguists) is a relatively recent phenomenon—just a few hundred years old. The "grandfather language" of English is Old English, the Anglo-Saxon dialect that conquering Germanic tribes brought with them to England in the fifth century A.D. (The word *English* is derived from *Angles,* the name of one of these conquering tribes.) Later, when William the Conqueror defeated the Germanic tribes at the Battle of Hastings (1066), he and his Norman conquerors brought with them a French influence. Allegorically, we might say that the English language's Anglo-Saxon grandfather married a French lady. The intermarried Germanic-French language that evolved from the eleventh to the fifteenth centuries is known as Middle English (Modern English's metaphorical father). Latin, the language of the church for centuries, also had some influence on the development of the English language.

History of the English Bible

While Latin was the official language of the church, a few portions of the Bible were translated into Old English (Anglo-Saxon) from the seventh to the eleventh centuries. In 1382, the famous reforming church leader John Wycliffe (1330–1384) translated the entire Bible into the English of his day (Middle English). The translation was based on the Latin Vulgate and was copied by hand, as the printing press had not yet been introduced to Europe.[1] Followers of Wycliffe continued to call for reform of the church and the monarchy, based on the biblical truth they were reading. Very quickly, church officials and the king judged the availability of the Bible in English as a threat to the status quo. In 1414, reading the Bible in English became a capital offense (that is, punishable by death). In 1428, Wycliffe's body was exhumed and symbolically burned at the stake.[2]

In 1526, William Tyndale (1494–1536) published the first *printed* (with a printing press) English New Testament, translated from the Greek original. Tyndale printed the New Testaments in continental Europe and smuggled them into England. The first complete printed English Bible appeared in 1535. It was called the Coverdale Bible because it was published under the leadership of Miles Coverdale, Tyndale's assistant. Tyndale was captured by followers of King Henry VIII, and in 1536, he was strangled and burned at the stake. As he was dying, Tyndale reportedly prayed, "Lord, open the eyes of the King of England." Only one year later, Tyndale's request was granted, as the king officially licensed the distribution of an English translation of the Bible. (See figure 7 for a summary of these early English Bible translations.) During the next hundred years, a spate of English Bible translations were produced, most of them heavily dependent on Tyndale's seminal work.

---

1. Europeans began using the printing press in 1454. The Chinese, however, were using printing presses long before Europeans.
2. Definitely the preferred way to be burned at the stake, as a friend once noted.

FIGURE 7: EARLY ENGLISH BIBLE TRANSLATIONS

DATE	WORK	DESCRIPTION
1382	Wycliffe Bible	First complete translation (handwritten) of the Bible into English based on the Vulgate.
1526	Tyndale Bible	First printed New Testament in English based on Greek.
1535	Coverdale Bible	First complete printed English Bible. Relies heavily on Tyndale Bible, German versions, and Vulgate.
1537	Matthew's Bible	Edited by John Rogers. Relies on Tyndale and Coverdale. First licensed English Bible.
1539	The Great Bible	Revised version of Matthew's Bible by Coverdale. Based on Tyndale, Hebrew, and Greek.
1560	Geneva Bible	The New Testament is a revision of Tyndale, and the Old Testament is revised based upon the Hebrew. First English Bible with verse divisions. Strongly Calvinistic footnotes.
1568	Bishops' Bible	A revision of the Great Bible translated by a committee of Anglican bishops.
1610	Douay-Rheims Bible	Literal rendering of the Vulgate by Roman Catholics.
1611	King James Version	Translated by a committee of scholars.

The Bible in Modern English

During the last one hundred years, and especially the last fifty, many good, reliable, and readable translations have been produced in English. Modern English speakers face a choice unlike any in the history of Bible translation. Rather than ask, "Which translation is best?" It is better to recognize that all translations have strengths and weaknesses. In fact, it is advisable for a Christian to own multiple Bible translations. The only Bible translations we can label as completely bad are those done by sectarian or cultic groups, such as the New World Translation (NWT), the Jehovah's Witness translation that attempts to remove scriptural teaching on the deity of Christ.

Approaches to Translation

There are two main approaches to Bible translation, and all translations fall somewhere along the spectrum between these two extremes (see figure 8). On one side is the functionally equivalent translation, sometimes called dynamically equivalent. This is a translation that seeks to accurately convey the same meaning in a new language but is not so concerned about preserving the same number of words or equivalent grammatical constructions. The New Living Translation (NLT) is a good example of a reliable functionally equivalent translation. On the other end of the spectrum is the formally equivalent translation. This type of translation is very concerned to preserve, as much as possible, the number of words and grammatical constructions from the original. Because languages are so different, a formally equivalent translation almost inevitably results in a stilted English style. The New American Standard Bible (NASB) and English Standard Version (ESV) are examples of formally equivalent translations. The New International Version (NIV) falls somewhere in the middle, being more functionally equivalent than the ESV but more formally equivalent than the NLT.

For reading larger portions of Scripture (reading through the Bible in one year, for example), a person might choose a functionally equivalent translation. For careful verse-by-verse study, one might prefer a more formally equivalent translation. In explaining a difficult passage to others in preaching or teaching, it is sometimes helpful to quote other Bible translations that clarify the meaning of the passage. Also, in personal study, reading a passage in multiple translations frequently results in increased comprehension. It is advisable to vary the Bible translation one reads to hear the text afresh.

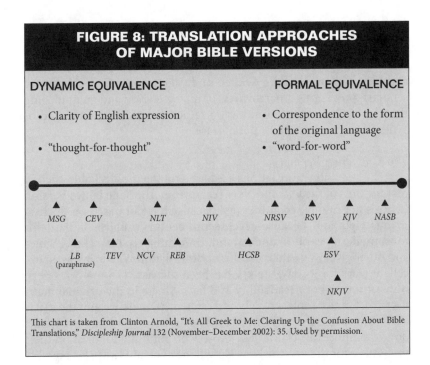

This chart is taken from Clinton Arnold, "It's All Greek to Me: Clearing Up the Confusion About Bible Translations," *Discipleship Journal* 132 (November–December 2002): 35. Used by permission.

Paraphrases

A paraphrase is not really a Bible translation but an attempt to freely word the meaning of the biblical text. A paraphrase is usually done by one person and allows for more interpretive comments than a functionally equivalent translation. Sometimes a paraphrase seeks to recast the biblical narrative in the setting of a certain subculture. *The Word on the Street*, a paraphrase by Rob Lacey, casts the Bible as "urban performance art." Clarence Jordan's famous paraphrase, *The Cotton Patch Version*, sets Jesus' ministry in the Southern United States of the 1950s, replacing Pharisees with white supremacists and Samaritans with African-Americans. *The Message*, by Eugene Peterson, seeks to clarify obscure passages and put them in the gritty language of everyday life.

The original Living Bible was a paraphrase of the American Standard Version (a formally equivalent translation completed in 1901) by Kenneth Taylor, which he composed for his children during his daily train commute.[3] (The New Living Translation, however, is not a paraphrase but a dynamically equivalent translation.) In contrast to paraphrases, Bible translations are always based on Greek and Hebrew texts and are worked on by large committees of diverse scholars, preventing a narrowness of interpretation and guaranteeing that the work remains a translation rather than veering into an idiosyncratic interpretation or paraphrase.

The King James Version

The best Bible translations are based on the most reliable ancient manuscripts of the Old and New Testaments. The King James Version (KJV) is not highly recommended because it is not based on the best manuscripts and because seventeenth-century English is hard for most modern people to understand. Unfortunately, many hotel Bibles and other giveaway Bibles are the KJV translation. While it was an excellent work for its day, the KJV has been surpassed by many modern translations in both readability and faithfulness to the original manuscripts. Some people wrongly and often passionately claim the KJV is a superior translation of the Bible. The historical and linguistic facts do not support this claim.[4] For those who continue to insist on their preference for the KJV, the New King James Version (NKJV) is possibly a better option—being based on the same manuscript tradition of the KJV but updated somewhat in language.

Recent Translation Debates

In recent years, conservative Bible translators have clashed over how to translate generic pronouns and similar constructions. For example, in older English, as well as ancient Greek, the pronoun *he* (or *autos*, in Greek) frequently was used to refer generically to both men and women. Fifty years ago, all English teachers would have said, "If a student wants to speak to me after class, *he* should stay in the room." Recently, there has been a move in English toward an informal generic "they" or "their" ("If a student wants to speak to me after class, *they* should stay in the room.") or the more cumbersome, "If a student wants to speak with me after class, *he or she* should stay in the room." Bible

---

3. Paul D. Wegner, *The Journey from Texts to Translations: The Origin and Development of the Bible* (Grand Rapids: Baker, 1999), 372–73.
4. See James R. White, *The King James Only Controversy: Can You Trust the Modern Translations?* 2nd ed. (Minneapolis: Bethany, 2009).

translators debate whether translating *autos* ("he") as "he or she" or *anthrōpos* ("man") as "person" faithfully conveys the meaning of the original. While the debate can be quite impassioned, the sides are closer than they appear, both acknowledging that much gender-specific language in the Bible was understood by the original recipients as applying to women too. For example, virtually all translators acknowledge that Paul's letters addressed to *adelphoi* ("brothers") in churches were in reality for all Christians, both men and women. The question remains, however, whether a Bible translation should render the expression *adelphoi* as "brothers and sisters" or "brothers." Is "brothers and sisters" an interpretation or translation? As one can see, this debate involves the distinction between formally and functionally equivalent translation theories. Scholars favoring the more gender-neutral translations are usually more inclined toward functionally equivalent translation theory. Those favoring a more strict correspondence of expressions are usually more disposed toward formally equivalent approaches to translation. Conservative, Bible-believing scholars, however, are agreed that Greek and Hebrew masculine pronouns for God should be rendered as masculine English pronouns ("he," "his" or "him") because God has revealed himself as Father.

REFLECTION QUESTIONS

1. Which version(s) of the Bible do you own? (Look in the first few pages of your Bible(s) to see.) Why do you use this Bible (or these Bibles)?

2. If your church has pew Bibles, what translation is it? Have you ever prejudged a person because of the Bible translation he or she preferred?

3. Do you prefer reading a more formally equivalent translation (word-for-word) or functionally equivalent translation (thought-for-thought)? Why?

4. If you were to obtain additional Bible translations to supplement your study, which ones would you get?

5. What translation of the Bible would you use for (a) careful, verse-by-verse study, (b) a gift to an international student, (c) reading through the Bible in one year with a group of college students?

FOR FURTHER STUDY

Brake, Donald L. *A Visual History of the English Bible: The Tumultuous Tale of the World's Bestselling Book.* Grand Rapids: Baker, 2008.

Fee, Gordon D., and Mark L. Strauss. *How to Choose a Translation for All Its Worth.* Grand Rapids: Zondervan, 2007.

Wegner, Paul D. *The Journey from Texts to Translations: The Origin and Development of the Bible.* Grand Rapids: Baker, 1999.

White, James R. *The King James Only Controversy: Can You Trust the Modern Translations?* 2nd ed. Minneapolis: Bethany, 2009.

www.biblegateway.com (free link to various Bible translations).

www.multilanguage.com (Bibles and Christian resources in languages other than English).

Select Bibliography

Archer, Gleason. *A Survey of Old Testament Introduction.* Rev. ed. Chicago: Moody Press, 1994.

Beale, G. K. *The Erosion of Inerrancy in Evangelicalism: Responding to New Challenges to Biblical Authority.* Wheaton, IL: Crossway, 2008.

Bruce, F. F. *The New Testament Documents: Are They Reliable?* 6th ed. Downers Grove, IL: InterVarsity Press; Grand Rapids: Eerdmans, 1981.

Carson, D. A. *For the Love of God: A Daily Companion for Discovering the Riches of God's Word.* Vols. 1 and 2. Wheaton, IL: Crossway, 1998, 1999.

_____. *New Testament Commentary Survey.* 6th ed. Grand Rapids: Baker, 2007.

Carson, D. A., and Douglas J. Moo. *An Introduction to the New Testament.* 2nd ed. Grand Rapids: Zondervan, 2005.

ESV Study Bible. Wheaton, IL: Crossway, 2008.

Evans, Craig A. *Fabricating Jesus: How Modern Scholars Distort the Gospels.* Downers Grove, IL: InterVarsity Press, 2008.

Fee, Gordon D., and Mark L. Strauss. *How to Choose a Translation for All Its Worth.* Grand Rapids: Zondervan, 2007.

Glynn, John. *Commentary and Reference Survey: A Comprehensive Guide to Biblical and Theological Resources.* 10th ed. Grand Rapids: Kregel, 2007.

Grudem, Wayne. *Systematic Theology: An Introduction to Biblical Doctrine.* Grand Rapids: Zondervan; Leicester: Inter-Varsity Press, 1994.

Longman, Tremper. *Old Testament Commentary Survey.* 4th ed. Grand Rapids: Baker, 2007.

Plummer, Robert L. *40 Questions About Interpreting the Bible.* Grand Rapids: Kregel, 2010.

Stein, Robert H. *A Basic Guide to Interpreting the Bible: Playing by the Rules.* 2nd ed. Grand Rapids: Baker, 2011.

Wegner, Paul D. *The Journey from Texts to Translations: The Origin and Development of the Bible.* Grand Rapids: Baker, 1999.

Zondervan NIV Study Bible, Rev. ed. Edited by Kenneth L. Barker, et al. Grand Rapids: Zondervan, 2008.

List of Figures